Differentiating for Inclusion

Target Ladders:
Sensory Processing

Inés Lawlor

Permission to photocopy

All rights reserved. This book contains materials which may be reproduced by photocopier or other means for use by the purchaser. The permission is granted on the understanding that these copies will be used within the educational establishment of the purchaser. The book and all its contents remain copyright. Copies may be made without reference to the publisher or the licensing scheme for the making of photocopies operated by the Publishers Licensing Society.

The right of Inés Lawlor to be identified as the author of this work has been asserted in accordance with Sections 77 and 78 of the Copyright, Designs and Patents Act 1988.

Target Ladders: Sensory Processing

ISBN: 978-1-85503-621-5

© Inés Lawlor 2017

Illustration © Robin Lawrie

This edition published 2017

10 9 8 7 6 5 4 3 2

Printed in the UK by Page Bros Ltd, Norwich

Designed and typeset by Andy Wilson for Green Desert Ltd

LDA, 2 Gregory Street, Hyde, Cheshire SK14 4HR

www.ldalearning.com

Contents

Introduction: Closing the gap	5
Sensory processing difficulties	7
What are sensory processing difficulties?	7
Sensory integration	14
Sensory Processing Disorder (SPD)	15
SPD and learning	18
Checklist to identify children with SPD	22
Sensory-friendly classroom	24
Creating a sensory-friendly classroom	24
Using Target Ladders	35
How to use this book	35
Records of Progress	40
The Target Ladders	
Aspect 1: Visual (sight)	44
Aspect 2: Auditory (hearing)	50
Aspect 3: Tactile (touch)	54
Aspect 4: Vestibular (movement and balance)	58
Aspect 5: Proprioception (body awareness)	62
Aspect 6: Gustatory and olfactory (taste and smell)	66
Aspect 7: Interoception (internal body functions and emotions)	68
Making changes brainstorming sheet template	70
References	71
Links to other *Target Ladders* titles	73
Other useful resources	74

All websites were correct at the time of going to press.

Closing the gap

Schools are committed to meeting the needs of children with Special Educational Needs and Disability (SEND). However, the range and complexity of needs encountered in mainstream primary schools continues to grow. The responsibility of identifying the needs, and of supporting class teachers in meeting those needs, lies with Special Educational Needs Co-ordinators (SENCOs), many of whom are class teachers themselves with limited experience of a wide variety of SENDs.

The Children and Families Act 2014 and the Special Educational Needs and Disability Code of Practice 2015 (CoP) both emphasise the importance of high aspirations for children with SEND. One indicator of the 'overall effectiveness' of a school will always be the extent to which the school meets the needs of pupils with SEND. Even if children are not formally recognised as having SEND, the school should still be able to provide evidence of action and intervention for those who are falling behind. School inspectors look for evidence that schools are working to 'close the gap' for all pupils who are not achieving age-related expectations. The first step in closing the gap is to identify what learners can do.

Case study

Hannah is a five-year-old girl who would frequently become upset and tearful in school. Close observation in the classroom and discussions with her parents indicated that she was very sensitive to touch. Her parents revealed that she found her school uniform uncomfortable, and it was very difficult to get her ready in the mornings. Her teacher observed that she was especially upset after PE class when she had to get changed back into her uniform. The teacher noted that she also became upset after transitions through the school, such as going to the playground. Understanding that the emotional outbursts might have been happening as a result of sensory overload enabled her parents and teacher to target the right areas to set goals for. Simple adjustments were made to the uniform (she was allowed not to wear the tie), and she was allowed to leave the classroom a few minutes ahead of the other children to minimise physical contact with them in the corridor. This enabled Hannah to be more relaxed and happy about going into school, and gradually she was able to progress through the Target Ladders to wearing the full uniform and joining the class when leaving the room to go out to play.

> ### Case study
> John is a six-year-old boy who has been diagnosed with autism. Although he is above average intelligence, he has difficulty in following basic instructions in the classroom and often doesn't complete his work. An assessment by his occupational therapist revealed difficulties with auditory processing (processing sounds).
> His teacher realised that he was unable to process verbal instructions in noisy environments. By making sure the class was quiet before giving instructions and also using visual cues to support what she was saying (in the form of a visual timetable), John was able to follow directions and meet his Target Ladder goals. He also wore sound-blocking headphones for concentrated pieces of work, and this allowed him to finish more quickly with less prompting than before.

Whether individual targets are recorded on an internal target sheet, a Record of Progress (RoP), a Pupil Passport or some other mechanism, the fact remains that children with SEND continue to need 'small steps' targets in order to clarify learning priorities and give them a sense of achievement when they tick off another target.

The SEND Code of Practice stresses the importance of teachers having a good understanding of individual SENDs and of using their best endeavours to ensure that a child with SEND gets the support they need. The *Target Ladders* series focuses on one SEND at a time, in order that the range of difficulties and challenges facing young people with that SEND can be acknowledged. A child does not, however, need to have a SEND to be helped by the targets and strategies mentioned in the book. If any child in your care has any of the behaviours or difficulties addressed by the book, then the targets and activities should be helpful and appropriate.

The *Target Ladders* series aims to support you by:

- focusing on what a child can do, rather than what they cannot do, in order to identify next steps;
- presenting 'small steps' targets for children;
- suggesting strategies and activities you may find helpful in order to achieve the targets;
- giving you the information you need to use your professional judgement and understanding of the child in determining priorities for learning;
- recognising that every child is different and will follow their own pathway through the targets;
- giving you an overview of the range of difficulties experienced by children with a particular SEND. Not all children will experience all of the difficulties, but once you know and understand the implications of a SEND, it gives you a better understanding as to a child's learning priorities.

Setting useful targets for a child can be tricky, but the process can be simplified if the exploration focuses on what the child *can* achieve rather than what they are not able to do. Once you know what a child can do, you are in a good position to set targets and consider interventions.

Using the *Target Ladders* series will enable non-specialist teachers to identify appropriate learning goals for independent learning, to adapt strategies or ideas listed and to begin to modify the learning difficulty to close the gap between these children and their peers.

What are sensory processing difficulties?

> No idea is conceived in our mind independent of our five senses (i.e. no idea is divinely inspired).
>
> Albert Einstein

Information from our senses tells us what is going on in the world and allows us to interact appropriately with our environment and the people in it. Although we are not aware of it, there is a constant stream of information being fed to our brains from all the senses. Our brains process and filter this stream, so we are only aware of sensory information that is perceived as important for us to pay attention to. For example, within a classroom there are numerous environmental sensory experiences going on at the same time, such as children chatting, chairs scraping on the floor, teachers walking along the corridor, bright lights and children moving around. If the child's ability to process this information is working well, their brain will filter out all the sensory information that is not important in order to allow them to listen to the teacher or concentrate on their activity. However, if the child has difficulty processing the information, they may perceive the other environmental stimuli, such as lights and other children, with equal intensity as the teacher's voice and therefore have difficulty following what the teacher is saying or attending to only one task.

Children with difficulty processing sensory information may therefore overperceive (notice too much) or underperceive (not notice) sensory signals. To others they may appear to overreact or underreact. However, the child's response is usually in proportion to what they are experiencing through their senses.

Before discussing sensory processing in more detail, we must first look at each of the senses and the role they play individually in children's development.

The sensory systems

Most people know about the first five senses: **visual** (sight), **auditory** (hearing), **tactile** (touch), **gustatory** and **olfactory** (taste and smell). However, there are also another three less commonly known senses. These are: our sense of movement and balance, known as the **vestibular** sense; our sense of body awareness, known as **proprioception**; and our sense of internal body function and emotional state, known as **interoception**.

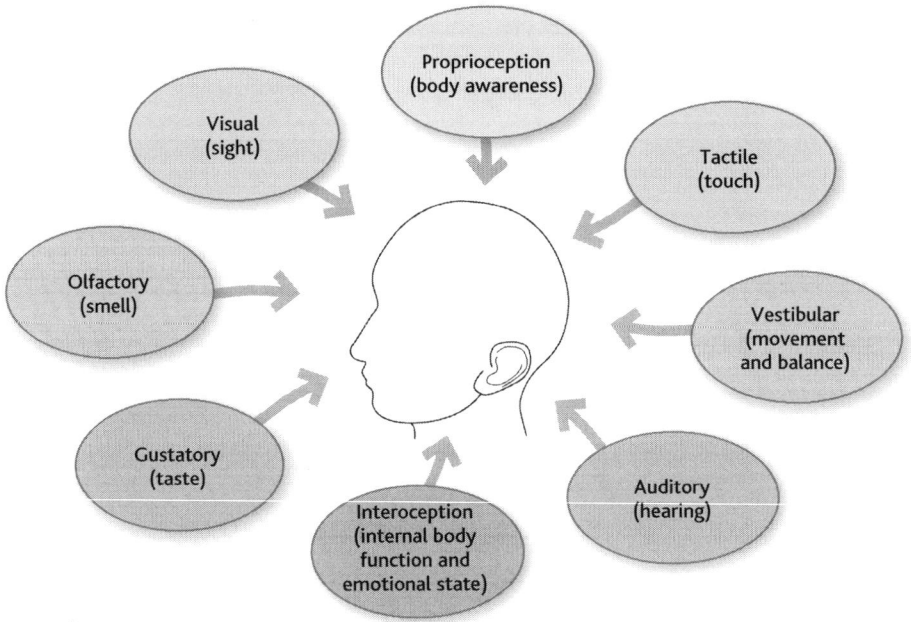

Fig. 1: The sensory systems.

Visual (sight)

The receptors for the visual system are the eyes. It is the sense we rely on most. For example, when we see something moving (such as the train on the platform next to us), we feel we must be moving, even though our other senses tell us we are still. The two eyes work together as a team, moving from side to side or up and down, to allow us to accurately scan the environment in front of us. Each eye sends an image to the brain, and these two images are then overlapped before the information is processed. To illustrate this, try putting your hands together in front of your face at arm's length, leaving a small gap. Look through the gap at one point in the distance. Then, close each eye in turn. You should notice that for one eye the image stays the same, but for the other you need to move your hands in order to see the focus point. So your brain is receiving two slightly different images but is able to process them so that you are only aware of one.

In order for the brain to accurately process the information, both eyes need to move together in all directions so that the two images match and are clear and not blurred. Co-ordinated use of the eyes develops as the child grows. During play and exploration, especially physical play that involves movement or objects which move, such as balls, the child's visual skills become more co-ordinated and efficient, making it easier for the brain to process the information. It is essential that young children, especially those under seven years, have regular daily opportunities for active free play, ideally outdoors, in order to develop these skills. By approximately age seven years a typically developing child should be able to focus on the board, focus on a page, track left to right when reading, throw and catch a ball with accuracy and move around their environment without crashing or bumping into things.

Children with poor eyesight or poor control of the muscles of the eyes (as opposed to difficulties processing visual information, see below) may have blurred or double vision, or be unable to track moving objects or sustain focus at the board or page. This can cause difficulties with attention, motor co-ordination, reading and writing and tolerance for different lighting conditions. It could be confused with a visual processing difficulty. It is therefore essential that all school-aged children have a thorough eye test by an optometrist or behavioural optometrist to rule out any underlying visual difficulty. (It is worth noting that the eye test needs to include both eyes working together: often children's eye tests only look at the focal length of each eye separately, which is not sufficient for classroom use. For more information see the British Association of Behavioural Optometrists – www.babo.co.uk) If a child has had their eyesight checked yet continues to have difficulty with recognising letters, copying from the board, reading, throwing and catching balls or finding objects on the desk, they may have a visual processing difficulty.

Difficulties processing visual information

The ability to process visual information allows us to recognise people, read facial expressions, judge the speed of a ball in order to catch it, judge the height of a step, focus on one thing in a busy environment and track words across a page. When we are reading, we can see in our periphery the person sitting next to us or the desk in the background, but we are still able to focus on the words on the page.

A child with visual processing difficulties may be unable to filter out the information that is not relevant. So, in a classroom where there are often many things and people to look at, the child may easily become distracted. Alternatively, they may have difficulty in registering or noticing visual input so may be unable to find things on their table or see that one letter is different from another.

Making eye contact or looking at people's faces can also be difficult for children with visual processing difficulties as the face contains many features which move when people talk, such as eyes, mouth, etc. The child may find it difficult to process all that information at once and therefore choose to look away and avoid eye contact.

Auditory (hearing)

The receptors for our auditory system are our ears. When we hear something, we are able to detect what type of sound it is, for example, a voice or a car alarm, and we can also tell which direction the sound is coming from. When a sound is on our right, we hear it with both ears, but the brain can detect that the signal from the right ear is stronger, so we know the sound must be on our right. To illustrate this, cover one ear and close your eyes. Ask someone to move around you and call your name. Notice how much more difficult it is to tell which direction the sound is coming from.

Another useful function of our auditory system is that is allows us to 'tune in' to useful information in noisy environments. For example, imagine yourself having a conversation with a friend in a cafe. Your auditory system is able to filter out other conversations in the background, the noise of the coffee machine and chairs moving, to allow you to focus on what your friend is saying.

Hearing loss (which may be caused by ear infections or fluid in the ear in conditions such as glue ear) can cause similar difficulties processing auditory information (see below). When a child has fluid in the ear, environmental sounds are distorted (like when you are under water), making language more difficult to understand. Children with fluid in the ear may also only hear sounds within a particular frequency, again missing parts of a sentence if the tone of voice changes beyond the frequency that is accessible to them. If the hearing loss is on only one side, the child will have difficulty localising sounds (knowing where it is coming from), so they will have to scan the environment to see who is talking. Children with fluid in the ear may also experience pain when exposed to particular sounds, causing them to cover their ears, potentially missing vital pieces of information in the classroom. Some children appear to be more prone to ear infections and fluid build-up in the ears than others and may have recurring, intermittent hearing loss of varying degrees over the early developmental years. During early childhood (aged 0–7 years), the brain is learning how to process information based on the information from the senses. If this information is inaccurate or inconsistent, this will make it more difficult for the brain to process the information accurately. Even when the hearing difficulty has resolved, some difficulty processing the information may persist as the brain has to 're-learn' how to process the sensory input from the auditory system with a new range of sounds. It is essential that all school-age children have a thorough hearing test, particularly if they seem to have sensitivity to noise, poor attention or difficulty following instructions.

Difficulties processing auditory information

A child with auditory processing difficulties will have difficulty with the filtering and interpretation of sounds carried to the brain from the ears. It is common for children with auditory processing difficulties to be sensitive to particular sounds, such as hand dryers, school bells or noisy environments like the playground or school hall. The child may also have difficulty in 'filtering out' background noise, such as another child talking or the sound of a distant lawnmower, and therefore have difficulty following what the teacher is saying. Alternatively, the child may not register certain sounds so may not respond when their name is called, or they may have difficulty following verbal instructions.

Tactile (touch)

The receptors for our tactile system are in our skin. Through our skin we can determine texture, pressure, temperature, pain, wet or dry, itch and tickle sensations. We also know which part of our body is being touched without having to look.

Because our skin is constantly touching something (such as clothing, the floor, a seat, the air), we are able to filter out those sensations that are not important (like the feel of our clothes) and only notice or attend to them if they change or become more important, for example, if we become too hot.

Difficulties processing tactile information

Children who have difficulty filtering and interpreting tactile sensations may be very sensitive to touch from others or to particular textures. They may find everyday sensations, such as the feel of their clothes, uncomfortable or even painful. This is sometimes termed 'tactile defensiveness'. Within a busy school environment this can be particularly difficult during arts and crafts where different textures are involved or when moving around the school where other children might bump into them. If the feel of their clothes is uncomfortable, the child will also have difficulty in attending to other tasks as their brain is continuing to respond to the feel of their clothes, so they may be irritable and more sensitive to other touch and more sensitive to pain. Alternatively, the child may not notice when their clothes are on the wrong way, their hands or face are messy or when someone taps them to get their attention. They may also need to 'seek out' more touch input in order to fully make sense of it. This may cause a problem if the child touches other children excessively or constantly fidgets with items on the table.

Children can also be sensitive to touch inside the mouth. They may dislike particular textures of food and having their teeth brushed. Combined with a sensitivity to the taste and smell of the food, this can cause children to have an extremely restricted diet. Over a period of time, poor diet can cause vitamin deficiencies and poor general health that may also contribute to difficulty with functioning in school.

Some children who have difficulty processing touch within the mouth may also chew or suck non-food objects in order to either stimulate an under-responsive sensory system or calm an over-responsive sensory system.

Gustatory (taste)

The receptors for our sense of taste are on our tongue. We can tell whether a food is sweet, salty, sour or bitter through our tongue. Additional information about the taste of the food comes from our sense of smell (olfactory sense). Our ability to taste is hugely linked to our sense of smell; we all know how tasteless food can be when we have a cold and a blocked nose.

We also have tactile receptors in our mouth that allow us to feel the texture, temperature, size and location of the food in our mouth.

Difficulties processing gustatory information

Children with difficulty in processing information from their gustatory system may be extremely sensitive to taste. A child who is sensitive to different tastes is likely to have a hugely restricted diet and will tend to limit their food to bland and consistent tastes. They will often be able to taste the difference between different brands of the same food. This can lead to long-term health risks, such as vitamin deficiencies and weight loss or gain.

Alternatively, a child with sensory processing difficulties may not register or recognise tastes and therefore might 'seek out' strong-tasting, spicy, excessively sweet or salty foods. Again, this may lead to long-term health problems. They may also put non-food objects in their mouth in an attempt to get more gustatory sensory input.

Within a classroom or school setting, difficulties with gustatory processing will mainly be an issue at mealtimes. The child may refuse to eat if the food available isn't to their sensory preferences. This can cause the child to be hungry and therefore struggle to maintain attention and be irritable as the day goes on (see **interoception** below).

Olfactory (smell)

The receptor for our sense of smell is our nose. Our sense of smell is extremely sensitive and helps us to recognise foods, objects, people and places. We interpret smells as pleasant or unpleasant. This helps protect us from harmful or toxic substances. Our sense of smell is also strongly linked to our memory (Addy, 2016) and shapes our perception of experiences.

Difficulties processing olfactory information

A child with difficulties processing olfactory information may be extremely sensitive to smells. Within the classroom they may dislike the smell of materials such as paint or playdough. The teacher's perfume or smell of washing powder on other children's clothes may cause distress. At mealtimes they may be unable to tolerate the canteen smell, or other people's lunch may cause them to gag or have to move away.

Alternatively, if a child has difficulty registering smell, it may cause them to 'seek out' strong smells or have to smell objects or people in order to be able to process the information accurately.

Vestibular (movement and balance)

The receptors for our vestibular system are in the inner ear. Our vestibular system detects changes in head position. We can tell, even with our eyes closed, in which direction we are moving and

Sensory Processing

at what speed, thanks to our vestibular system. Our vestibular system is constantly monitoring which position our head is in and then sends signals to the muscles of the body to make small adjustments in order to keep us balanced and upright.

To illustrate, try standing up tall and shift your weight over to the right. You should feel the muscles on your right side contract slightly in order to bring you back into the centre and stop you from falling over. The tightness of the muscles around a joint when at rest is known as 'muscle tone'. Your muscle tone increases (your muscles contract) to keep you balanced and upright. This is regulated by your vestibular system.

If you continue to move to the right whilst standing, you become more off balance; you need more than just small adjustments in muscle tone to stop you from falling over. Firstly, you would put out your hands and eventually take a step to the right to save yourself. These reactions are termed 'balance reactions'.

The vestibular and visual systems also work together to stop you from getting dizzy when moving. When we move our heads in one direction, our eyes move in the opposite direction in order to keep the image as stable as possible and therefore easy to interpret. Our eyes can also move independently from our head in order to track an object from left to right. In order for the visual and vestibular systems to work well together, both systems need to be working well independently, and they need to be communicating well together.

During everyday activities, even if we are relatively still (such as seated at a desk), small movements of our head (triggering our vestibular system) will send messages to the brain to tell us where we are. Our body will automatically adjust, without us having to think about it, to help us remain balanced. This means our brain can attend more easily to the task in front of us.

Difficulties processing vestibular information

Children who have difficulty processing vestibular information may over-respond or under-respond to movement. If their sensory system overperceives vestibular signals, they may fear movement such as walking on unstable surfaces (like sand), walking up or down hills or steps or standing on moving playground equipment. Alternatively, their sensory system may not perceive cues from their vestibular system, leading to low muscle tone and delayed balance reactions.

If their vestibular system is not registering the position of the head with an average amount of movement, the child may need to 'seek out' more movement in order to get the input the brain needs. This can result in the child fidgeting, rocking on their chair, moving off their chair frequently or seeking more intense input, such as spinning. In addition to this, if the child is having to use the thinking part of their brain to balance on the chair (something which should be automatic), it will make attending to other tasks more difficult and tiring, so the child may also show poor attention.

Proprioception (body awareness)

The receptors for our proprioceptive sense are located in our muscles and joints. They are triggered when we move and stretch. Our proprioceptive system allows us to detect where our body is without having to look. To illustrate this, try closing your eyes and touching your nose. It is our proprioceptive system that enables us to move our arms with reasonable accuracy, even when our vision is occluded.

This is useful for every activity we participate in. If we had to look at our arms and legs when we were walking, we wouldn't be able to look where we were going, making it very difficult not to bump into things and trip over!

Difficulties processing proprioceptive information

If a child has difficulty with registering or processing sensory input from the proprioceptive system, they will have a poor sense of where their body is. The child may therefore have difficulty co-ordinating the body during movement or have a poor sense of personal space. The child may also 'seek out' more body awareness. This might be through activities such as bumping and crashing, stretching or moving more than their peers.

Interoception (internal body functions and emotions)

The receptors for our interoceptive system are located in most of the tissues of our body: organs, muscles, skin, bones, etc. Our interoceptive system gives us a sense of hunger or fullness, nausea or pain internally, the need to go to the toilet and how we are feeling emotionally (Mahler, 2016). Accurate interoception allows us to notice and give meaning to sensations. For example, when we feel a rumbling in our stomach and our mouth is watering, we know we are hungry. When we feel our heart beating and a churning feeling in our stomach, we interpret this as feeling anxious.

Difficulties processing interoceptive information

A child who has with difficulty registering and processing interoceptive information may be extremely sensitive to internal body sensations. In the case of elimination, the child may become extremely distracted or agitated if they need to go to the toilet.

Alternatively, a child may have difficulty in registering or attaching meaning to sensations. They may not realise they need the toilet until it is too late, or they may not notice they are becoming upset until they are at the point of a meltdown.

Sensory integration

In order to function effectively within our environment, our body processes information from each of the senses individually *and* collectively. For example, when we walk, all our senses work together so we can navigate our way effectively. Our eyes help us assess the environment, our vestibular sense keeps us balanced, our sense of touch is assessing the stability and texture of the floor, our proprioceptive sense tells us how our legs are moving, our hearing, smell and taste senses will be alert to any potential risks, and our interoception will monitor how we are feeling, so we can attend to the task of walking without falling over. The complex balancing, sorting and filtering of sensory information is termed 'sensory integration'.

Sensory Integration theory was first described by Dr Jean Ayres in 1972. Ayres defined sensory integration as 'the neurological process that organises sensation from one's own body and from the environment and makes it possible to use the body effectively within the environment' (Ayres 1972 cited in Bundy, Lane & Murray, 2002).

Bundy, Lane & Murray describe sensory integration as a circular process similar to that below:

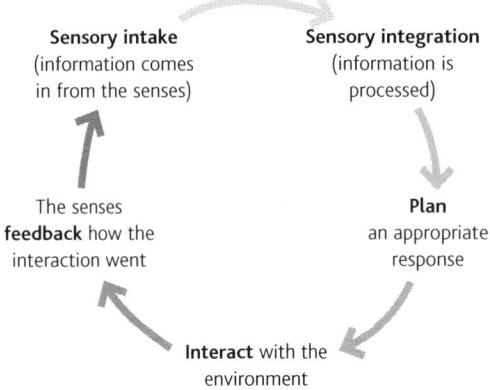

Fig. 2: Sensory integration. Adapted from Fig.1.1 p. 5 Bundy, Lane & Murray (2002).

As can be seen from the diagram above, there is a continuous communication between the body (through the senses) and the environment. For example, a child hears a bell ringing in the classroom, the brain processes it and identifies it as the bell for break time. The child then plans to put on their coat and line up at the door (or whatever is the routine in the class). They then carry out the plan and their senses will feedback whether this was the right thing to do; for example, they can see other children doing the same. However, if the child had difficulty in processing what the sound was, or didn't register it at all, the cycle would break down. This would be potentially confusing for them as they can only form a plan with the information they have from their senses. If this is inaccurate, the outcome is likely to be inaccurate too.

Sensory Processing Disorder (SPD)

Diagnosis

Despite the fact that the term 'Sensory Processing Disorder' (SPD) is widely used, it is currently not recognised in the *Diagnostic and Statistical Manual of Mental Disorders* (DSM-5™) (American Psychiatric Association, 2013), which is widely used as a touchstone for diagnostic practices. Therefore, clinicians can be reluctant to officially use the term 'disorder' and prefer to say sensory processing 'difficulties' or 'differences', or the child may be described as having 'sensory issues'. Although these different terms can be confusing, it is always more helpful anyway to look at the child's individual needs, rather than focus on the diagnostic criteria, so it is not a concern for the purposes of intervention. For the purposes of this discussion, 'SPD' will be used to represent Sensory Processing Disorder/Difficulties/Differences.

A suitably trained occupational therapist can confirm that a child's sensory processing is significantly different to that expected for their age and developmental level. Usually, this is done through a series of questionnaires such as the Sensory Processing Measure (SPM) (Parham et al, 2007) or the Sensory Profile 2™ (Dunn, 2015). Both these measures ask the parent and the teacher to rate the frequency of observable behaviours that may indicate SPD. These can be plotted on a chart to give a summary of which sensory areas the child is showing particular difficulty with, compared to their peers.

An occupational therapist working with the child may also choose to administer further objective testing and standardised tests to assess the child's sensory, motor or perceptual skills in more detail.

Categories of SPD

SPD is sub-categorised by occupational therapists as shown below:

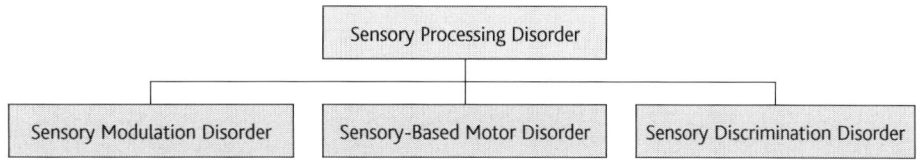

Fig. 3: Adapted from Miller et al (2007a) in Addy L (2016).

Sensory Discrimination Disorder describes the ability to differentiate the subtle differences and properties of sensory input in one particular sense, for example, the ability to discriminate visually between the letters *d* and *b* or the ability to hear different tones of voice to determine if the person is angry or sad.

Sensory-Based Motor Disorder describes a difficulty in performing motor tasks as a result of poor sensory processing.

Sensory Modulation Disorder describes difficulties with regulating sensory input and the ability to remain engaged and alert during tasks. Generally, if a child is described as having Sensory Processing Disorder or Sensory Processing Difficulties, it is likely to be a difficulty with sensory modulation.

Prevalence of SPD

Due to the inconsistency of terminology used to diagnose SPD and the overlap with other conditions, there are currently no definitive statistics for the prevalence of SPD in the UK population. Miller (2014) states that current research in the USA indicates the prevalence to be at least five per cent of kindergarten-aged children show significant difficulties with sensory processing, and the prevalence could be as high as 16 per cent. This equates for at least one child in every classroom of 30 children.

Although there is a correlation with other conditions (see below), SPD symptoms have also been shown to exist without the child meeting any other diagnostic criteria (Van Hulle et al & Carter et al in Miller, 2014), thus further validating the existence of SPD as a distinct condition.

Causes of SPD

The exact cause of SPD, like many other childhood conditions, is unknown. However, several risk factors have been implicated. Prenatal and birth complications, genetic heredity, institutionalised care in early childhood and maternal stress and alcohol consumption during pregnancy are the most commonly implicated (Miller, 2014).

There is also an emerging body of evidence suggesting recent changes in lifestyle may account for the increase in children with 'sensory issues' within the classroom. Hanscom (2016) advocates that school-aged children (5–13 years) need at least four to five hours of physical activity and outdoor play daily. With an increase in families where both parents are working outside of the home and a preference for more sedentary play, such as video games, it is unlikely that most of the children in an average classroom are getting even half this amount. As we will discuss below, sensory processing is the core on which other skills are built. Sensory processing in neurotypical children requires stimulation of *all* the senses. Free physical play, in particular outdoors where the environment is less predictable (hence providing more challenges) and less over-stimulating, provides opportunities for this. Long periods sitting down or in a sensory-poor environment do not provide these opportunities and can result in an inefficient or overreactive sensory system.

Correlation with other conditions

Children who have other diagnoses sometimes also exhibit signs of poor sensory processing. Being on the autism spectrum or having Attention Deficit Hyperactivity disorder (ADHD) are the most common conditions associated with SPD symptoms. Children with other conditions including Fragile X syndrome, Cerebral Palsy, Visual Impairment, Moderate Learning Difficulties and Down's syndrome (Roley, Blanche & Schaaf, 2001) also display behaviours associated with poor sensory processing.

Autism and SPD

Difficulty in processing sensation is extremely common in children on the autism spectrum. It is estimated that up to 90 per cent of children with autism have SPD (Miller, 2014). In fact, the DSM-5™ includes sensory issues as part of the diagnostic criteria for Autism Spectrum Disorder (ASD) as follows:

> Hyper- or hypo-reactivity to sensory input or unusual interests in sensory aspects of the environment (e.g. apparent indifference to pain/temperature, adverse response to specific sounds or textures, excessive smelling or touching of objects, visual fascination with lights or movement).

(www.autismspeaks.org/what-autism/diagnosis/dsm-5-diagnostic-criteria)

Children with autism, like all children, are individuals, so each child will have their own set of sensory preferences. However, there are common trends identified in children with autism with regard to sensory processing. Taste, smell, auditory and touch sensitivities are extremely common (Myles et al, 2000), as are under-responsivity in the vestibular and proprioceptive senses leading to poor motor and organisational skills (Miller, 2014).

It is also hypothesised that some repetitive and stereotyped behaviours seen in children with autism (such as hand flapping), may be an attempt by the child to provide themselves with the sensory input they need to self-regulate their level of arousal (Gabriels, Agnew & Miller, 2008).

Attention Deficit Hyperactivity Disorder (ADHD) and SPD

There is a huge overlap between behaviours that exist in ADHD and those which are common in SPD. For example, it is common for children with SPD to have difficulty sitting still, due to poor vestibular and proprioceptive processing, poor posture or sensitivity to touch or sounds. Difficulty sitting still and constant movement are also a core feature of ADHD. Therefore, it is common for children with SPD to be misdiagnosed with ADHD. Preliminary research suggests that both conditions are different but also can co-exist (Miller, Nielsen & Schoen, 2012). Approximately 40 per cent of children diagnosed with ADHD also display SPD (Miller, 2014).

Again, an individualised approach is most beneficial in deciding goals for a child, rather than one based on the diagnosis.

SPD and learning

Effective sensory integration is the core skill on which all other learned skills are built (see Fig. 4 below). If the brain cannot process the information that it receives from the senses with accuracy, this impacts the child's ability to move their body effectively. If they can't move their body effectively, their ability to manipulate objects and explore their environment will be impaired. This will have a further impact on the development of language and social skills and emotional development. Finally, if all the other areas of development are delayed, this will make academic learning more difficult.

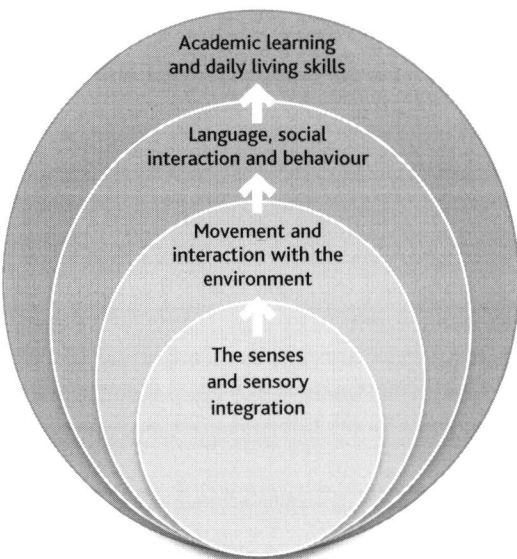

Fig. 4: Sensory integration.

For example, a child who has difficulty in processing tactile information may find touch from others irritating. Therefore, in the playground they may avoid moving so as not to accidentally bump into another child. In doing so, they are limiting the development of their balance and co-ordination due to creating fewer opportunities to practise these skills. They may also miss opportunities to play with others, thus missing out on opportunities to learn language and communication skills. Finally, they will have missed an opportunity to develop social skills such as turn taking, winning and losing, or perhaps maths skills if the game involves keeping a score.

Another child with visual processing difficulties may become easily distracted by other children's heads and movement of their peers during carpet time. They therefore might find sitting still and looking at the teacher difficult. Hence, they may miss key pieces of vocabulary from the teacher as well as missing a potential opportunity to express their own opinion and the language and learning that occurs from this.

As you can see from these examples, what seems like a small sensory difficulty can have a knock-on effect on the child's overall development and learning.

SPD: attention and alertness

Filtering of sensory information allows us to maintain an appropriate level of arousal/alertness and attention to the task we are performing (Lane, 2002). In order to attend, we need to be neither over-alert nor under-alert. Our level of alertness or arousal is determined by the amount of sensory input we receive and how our brain processes it. An example of feeling 'over-alerted' by sensory input might be going Christmas shopping in crowded, overheated shops. We would receive more tactile input from brushing past people as we chose what to buy. Christmas music blaring would stimulate our auditory sense, and the cluttered shelves and Christmas decorations and lights would be highly stimulating to our visual sense. Most of us can imagine the feeling of **sensory overload** in this scenario, our sensory system being so saturated with sensory input that it could no longer process any more. Usually this would result in irritability, and we would choose to go home at that point. In a child, the reaction might be a 'sensory meltdown', where the child feels overwhelmed by the environment, becomes angry, very upset or runs away. Stress (including sensory stress from sensory overload) triggers the release of adrenaline in our brain which leads to responses of flight, fight, or freeze and eventually to shut down. As adults, our interoception (awareness of emotional and physical state) generally enables us to recognise the onset of sensory overload and to plan an action in response; children with SPD haven't yet learned to 'read' their bodies and often become quickly overwhelmed. When we become 'too alert', or hyper-reactive, paying attention and learning new information becomes very difficult. In this 'fight or flight' state our body is focused only on survival and how to escape the environment or situation which is presenting us with a perceived threat. Therefore, our capacity to attend to new information is reduced.

Becoming under-alert, or hypo-reactive, equally affects our ability to attend to tasks. An example of when we might feel under-alert is perhaps first thing on a Monday morning when we are returning to work after a busy weekend. We may find conversations more difficult to follow, our organisational skills and movements may be slightly slower, and we may feel irritable towards others or in general. In circumstances like this, we may choose to walk to work, drink a caffeinated drink or turn on the radio in order to 'wake up' our sensory system and become more alert by the time we need to begin work. When a child's sensory system is under-alert they may need stimulation, often through movement, in order to wake them up and engage them.

Whether under- or over-alert, all of us use self-regulation strategies in order to try and get the optimal level of alertness for the task we are engaged in (Williams & Shellenberger, 1996). This means that we all continuously seek out sensory activities that help us maintain this optimal level of alertness. For example, when we are feeling overloaded, we may need to have a hot bath (tactile), do some yoga or other exercise we find relaxing (vestibular and proprioceptive), eat something sweet (gustatory), or go somewhere quiet (auditory) in order to meet our sensory needs and feel 'just right' again. Conversely, we may seek out alerting sensory input if we are becoming under-alert.

For most of us, a subtle or small sensory activity is enough to allow us to maintain the optimal level of alertness and stay on task. For example, if we are listening to a long talk and feel ourselves becoming under-alert we may shift our sitting position slightly or even take notes. This gives our vestibular and tactile systems a 'boost' of sensory input which also boosts our level of alertness so we can remain on task. However, everybody is different. Some people need more sensory input to 'wake up' their sensory system. Others are more sensitive to sensation and need only a little to become too overloaded.

This is the same in *all* children too. Within every classroom, each child will have their own unique way of processing sensation and therefore their own set of sensory preferences. Whilst still within the average range, some children will be more sensitive to sensation and others will need more sensation to attend.

Children who have SPD (or other conditions with sensory processing difficulties as a feature of the condition) may have an exceptionally low threshold for sensation, so they quickly become 'too alert' or, on the other end of the sensory spectrum, they may require more sensory input than others to function efficiently. The average classroom environment may not provide the right balance of sensory input to allow children with SPD to perform tasks to the best of their abilities. Occupational therapist Patricia Wilbarger (1984) coined the term 'sensory diet' to describe the use of sensory activities interspaced at regular intervals throughout the day to allow the individual to maintain the optimal level of alertness.

Emotional regulation

When we are too alert from an excess of sensory input, it is likely that we also feel more emotional. How we feel depends on the circumstances; sometimes we may feel irritable, at other times we may feel close to tears or anxious. Our emotions are invariably heightened when we feel overloaded due to the strong connections in the brain between the areas that process sensation and our emotional centre (Lane, 2002).

In addition to this, when we feel emotional, our ability to process sensation is affected. As discussed, if we are anxious or stressed, our body reacts with a 'fight or flight' response (Williams & Shellenberger, 1996). Imagine walking on a quiet street at night and hearing a sound behind you. Your sensory system would immediately become more alert; that is, you would look around for signs of danger, listen for more noise, etc. Then, if you felt someone tap you on the shoulder you may either run (flight), or turn around to face your assailant (fight). In other circumstances a touch on the shoulder would probably not make you react in the same way. In other words, we become more sensitive to sensation when we are anxious or stressed. Similarly, within a classroom, if a child is anxious or stressed, they are more likely to overperceive sensory input. So, if they are touched on the shoulder, they may become excessively upset or aggressive as they perceive the sensation as threatening. The brain doesn't distinguish between perceived threats and real threats; the body just reacts. To an onlooker it may seem like an overreaction, but to the child it seems in proportion to what they are experiencing.

Having SPD can therefore become a cycle of emotional and sensory sensitivity (see Fig. 5). For example, a child with SPD may be sensitive to noise and dislike the noise of the school hall during assembly. The next time the child is brought to assembly they are already anxious about the imminent sensory experience as they remember it as unpleasant from last time. Therefore, being anxious makes them more sensitive to the noise which in turn makes the experience more unpleasant than the last time, and the cycle continues with increasing intensity.

In summary, children with sensitivity to sensation are more likely to be emotionally sensitive (e.g. anxious or prone to 'meltdowns') and, vice versa, children who are emotional for any reason (e.g. upset, anxious, frustrated) will be more sensitive to sensation.

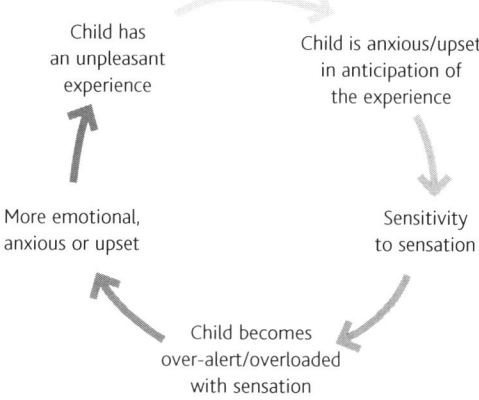

Fig. 5: Sensitivity and anxiety.

It is also important to note that sensory input has a cumulative effect; that is, it builds up over the course of the day. This is why a loud noise at 10am may be tolerable but we may be irritated by the same volume of noise at 4pm. Children with SPD can often appear inconsistent in their responses to sensation as at certain times they may tolerate a sensation and at others become overwhelmed by it. Remember that the child's reaction is *always* in proportion to what they are perceiving (which comes from information from the senses). Depending on the other sensory experiences they have had during the day, whether they had any opportunities for 'self-regulation' and how they feel emotionally, the same sensory experience may be tolerable one day and unbearable the next.

Checklist to identify children with SPD

As discussed, there are standardised questionnaires to screen for SPD. These are usually issued, scored and interpreted by the child's occupational therapist. The checklist below is therefore not intended to diagnose SPD, rather to assist you in determining which children may require further assessment for SPD. One behaviour in isolation does not necessarily indicate SPD, but a cluster of behaviours or multiple across the senses might and warrants further assessment. If you answer 'yes', when compared to same-age peers, to several behaviours in the checklist, you may wish to discuss with the child's parents whether or not to seek additional advice from an occupational therapist.

Visual (sight)	Yes/No
Has poor/decreased eye contact during social interactions	
Has difficulty in maintaining visual attention to tabletop work	
Has difficulty in tracking moving objects or people	
Seems bothered by lights or changes in lighting conditions	
Has poor hand–eye co-ordination during ball games	
Has difficulty copying from a board or sheet of paper with accuracy	
Has difficulty finding things in a cluttered space	
Auditory (hearing)	
Has difficulty tolerating everyday sounds	
Has difficulty in following verbal instructions	
Has difficulty in regulating volume or tone of voice when speaking	
Covers ears or becomes distressed in noisy environments	
Is easily distracted by background noise	
Misunderstands or has incomplete recall of what has been said	
Tactile (touch)	
Has extreme dislike of touch from others	
Constantly fidgets with objects in hands	
Has difficulty in grading force when handling objects	
Extremely dislikes or refuses to touch particular textures, such as paint, playdough	
Tries to avoid standing in lines or groups near other children who might bump them	
Has extreme dislike of, or becomes upset at, getting hands or face dirty	

Has difficulty tolerating school uniform or other items of clothing	
Doesn't notice when clothes are twisted or not on correctly	
Has an unusually high or low pain threshold	
Harms/hurts themselves through repeated sensory-seeking behaviours (e.g. biting or pinching own hands, head-banging)	
Has difficulty with fine motor tasks, including dressing	
Vestibular (movement and balance)	
Constantly seeks movement	
Is excessively cautious/fearful of movement	
Has poor posture	
Has poor balance during everyday movement	
Proprioception (body awareness)	
Has poor motor co-ordination (e.g. trips frequently, bumping into people/objects)	
Appears to deliberately bump, crash, lean on objects/people excessively	
Has difficulty maintaining appropriate personal space with others	
Plays too roughly with peers	
Applies too much or too little pressure on the page when writing or drawing	
Walks on toes only	
Gustatory and olfactory (taste and smell)	
Has extreme dislike of environmental smells	
Gags or becomes upset at particular tastes or smells	
Constantly chews or bites non-food items	
Interoception (internal body functions and emotions)	
Has difficulty regulating emotions	
Has excessive hunger/thirst	
Has frequent toileting 'accidents', more than expected for age	
Issues related to behaviour as a result of poor sensory processing	
Is more anxious/fearful than their peers	
Dislikes changes in routine	
Has difficulty relating to peers	

Creating a sensory-friendly classroom

A sensory-friendly classroom is a learner-friendly classroom and will help all students within the class. As we have learned so far, *all* children process sensation in different ways. Creating an environment that caters to a range of sensory preferences will make the classroom more pleasant for everyone (including the teacher!).

Sensory over- or under-alertness is usually a mismatch between the person and the environment. Therefore, when creating a sensory-friendly environment, we need to consider both strategies that adapt/prepare the child for the classroom and strategies that adapt/prepare the classroom for the child.

Classroom environment

Seating

It is common for children with SPD to have difficulties sitting at a table for long periods of time. This may be due to low muscle tone (affecting their posture), difficulty processing vestibular and proprioceptive sensations (they need more movement to register the sensory input), or they may be in 'flight' mode if feeling overloaded by sensations.

The ideal seated position for all children is with their feet flat on the floor, with hips and knees at 90 degree angles. The seat length should allow the child to make contact with the backrest. The desk should be at about elbow height in this position. This allows the body to be relaxed but supported to allow the fine motor movements of the arms and hands for writing (Landy & Burridge, 1999). As children come in different sizes, chairs and tables should be different sizes too. Ideally, there should be a range of different chair heights so children can put their feet on the ground flat for support. If they can't reach the ground, they are likely to either slide forward on their seat to touch the ground or wrap their legs around the chair legs for support. If there isn't an option to have a variety of chair heights, use books or boxes under the feet of children who can't reach the ground – but beware of health and safety implications and creating tripping hazards. School chairs with arm rests (if available) also provide more support.

Consider allowing the children to work in different positions for different activities throughout the day, for example, painting at an easel or playing with playdough when standing at the table.

Some children may work better lying down on the carpet area where their body is fully supported and they get more feedback from their tactile system from the floor. This might be suitable for reading or colouring activities.

If a child has difficulty in sitting still on the carpet, try using beanbags (which provide more tactile input), or coloured cushions or carpet squares, so each child has a visual marker for their own space (Biel & Peske, 2009).

Specialised seating

Some children may need more supportive seating, such as a chair with arm rests, a foot support or a higher back, in order to be able to maintain an upright posture. These will usually be recommended by the occupational therapist involved with the child.

For children who need more movement than average to maintain attention in sitting, products such as the Movin' Sit cushion or a ball seat (www.ldalearning.com) can provide movement whilst the child remains seated. The child's occupational therapist will usually recommend these products also.

It is advisable that any specialised seating is reviewed regularly as the child grows to ensure the dimensions and type of seating are still suitable.

Movement breaks

Hanscom (2016) recommends school-aged children are allowed 4–5 hours a day of unstructured physical play to develop a healthy sensory system. This will have to be divided between the time the child is in school and the time they are at home. Talk with parents about the need for movement throughout the day, so children have lots of opportunities to move outside of school, as this will have a knock-on effect for their attention in school. Ask parents if it is possible for the child to walk, scoot or cycle to school as it will help the child feel calmer from the start of the day. After school, children should also be given opportunities to move, for example, go to parks, playgrounds, swimming or play in the garden if possible.

Consider opening the playground before school starts, so children can run around for 10–15 minutes at the start of the day, or offering a structured movement programme before school.

Within the school day, all children benefit from regular movement breaks about every 20–40 minutes (O'Connor, 2012). This aids learning for all children as it provides proprioceptive and vestibular input which helps maintain the optimal level of alertness. This can be done within the classroom. Simply moving to different workstations or giving a child a 'job' such as handing out books may be sufficient. Other children may need to be given extra breaks out of the classroom such as taking a message to another class or being allowed extra time on the playground.

Some schools have purchased a trampoline, and the child is given the opportunity to jump on it outside of the classroom at regular intervals as agreed with the teacher.

Sensory games and activities

Movement and balance

As well as regular movement breaks, children with SPD will benefit from a range of sensory games and activities which can easily be incorporated into PE activities for the whole class. Movement games will help children with gross motor skills, balance, body awareness, co-ordination and tolerance for touch and tactile experiences as well as developing confidence and strengthening peer relationships – and being fun! (Many more games and activities are included in the Target Ladders on pages 44–69).

- **Popcorn maker.** Usually, slow predictable movements such as rocking or jumping up and down are easier to tolerate than fast unpredictable movements such as spinning. Rocking in the chair can be achieved with this 'popcorn maker' game (Henry D, 2000) Ensure there is enough space for the child to rock forwards without banging their head on the table or another person.
  - Sit in a chair with your feet flat on the floor.
  - Use your hands and feet to help push you up and down in a rhythmical fashion.
  - Start slowly and build up to more quickly as the child's tolerance for movement increases.
- **Movement programmes.** Teachers in some schools undergo additional training in children's yoga which can be incorporated into the school curriculum and provide movement as part of academic subjects or as small movement breaks to aid learning. Movement programmes such as SMART Moves (www.smartcc.co.uk/smart-smartmoves.html) or Brain Gym® (www.braingym.org.uk) might also be useful for your school to improve motor skills whilst providing vestibular sensory input if needed for particular pupils. Sensory Circuits (www.ldalearning.com) can also be useful and can be adapted to meet individual children's sensory needs.
- **What am I?** Use pictures of animals, professions, hobbies, etc. and ask the child to mirror the position with their body. This could also be done with letters and the child could spell a word.
- **Wacky races.** Race from one end of the room to the other in different positions (e.g. commando crawling, bottom shuffling, kneeling, all fours, etc.).
- **Atoms.** Ask the children to move around the room slowly at first, trying not to bump into each other. If they touch another child, those two children have to hold hands. Gradually decrease the size of the space the children have to move around so it becomes more difficult to move without touching. For more body awareness games see Sensory Shuffle (www.ldalearning.com).
- **Tightrope.** Use chalk (or use coloured tape or skipping ropes) to mark out a line on the ground. Practise balancing on the line. Roll a dice: 1 = slow walking, 2 = fast walking, 3 = heel to toe, 4 = hopping, 5 = tip toes, 6 = backwards.
- **Obstacle courses.** Create a simple obstacle course from PE equipment. Obstacle courses that involve several changes of position will challenge the child's balance more than if they are in the same position throughout. For example:
  - use bean bags to create stepping stones;
  - commando crawl under a gym mat;
  - walk across a bench;
  - hop around cones placed in a zigzag pattern;
  - jump over bean bags with two feet together;
  - balance heel to toe along a line.

Ask the child to create their own obstacle course as this will motivate them to keep practising it for longer.
- **Practise at home.** Consider asking parents to practise particular motor skills at home to further improve the child's skills.

Force for writing

Children with SPD often experience challenges with writing or drawing as they find it hard to judge how much pressure to put on the pencil, typically using too much or too little force.

- **Soft, silicone tubular pencil grips** (www.ldalearning.com) can help reduce the pressure children use to hold their pencils and reduce the likelihood of children finding writing hard because their hands ache.
- **Interleaving carbon paper** between sheets of different coloured paper – or using an office receipts book – can help to give children feedback as to the requisite amount of force to use when writing. Challenge them to write so that it can be seen only through one piece of carbon paper.
- **Correct pressure.** Use different types of paper so the child can observe and discuss which needs more or less pressure so as not to tear (e.g. try writing on tissue paper, aluminium foil, cardboard).
- Ask the child to **self-check**. Teach them how to tell the difference between too hard and too light. After a piece of writing, give the child a green pen and ask them to mark all the words that are 'just right' pressure.

(More suggestions to improve force for writing are given in the Target Ladders on pages 44–69.)

Visual

If the child is very sensitive to visual sensation they may find it easier to attend in a clutter-free environment. Think about the visual stimulation in the room.

- **Clutter-free room.** Wall displays and hanging ceiling displays are beautiful, but they can be very attractive to the eye and difficult for a child with SPD to ignore. Try to keep visual displays of work on the wall in the line of the child's vision to a minimum. Individual work stations can be created using a large cardboard box cut in half, or specially made privacy boards can be purchased (www.ldalearning.com) to give the child a totally distraction-free workspace if needed.
- **Clutter-free table.** Keep table clutter to a minimum. If a child is required to attend to a page on the table, remove other items from the table.
- **Position.** Think about the position of the child in the room in relation to the area where you want them to look. If they are sitting sideways on to you but facing another child, they may find it difficult to ignore the other child and look towards you, or concentrate on their work. Some children benefit from a completely distraction-free environment to work in. You might have a corner in the room where you can create this, or a privacy board (www.ldalearning.com) could be used for times when the child wants to concentrate on a piece of work.
- **Lighting.** Natural lighting conditions (rather than fluorescent lights) are easier to tolerate for children who are sensitive, so try seating the child near a window.

- **Table lamp.** Some opticians recommend using LED/halogen table lamps shining directly on the child's work. The table lamp is brighter than a fluorescent strip light and mitigates the shimmering impact of the strip light. Be aware of health and safety considerations, however, so the child cannot trip over an electrical lead or burn themselves on a hot light.
- **Colour coding.** Children who have difficulty registering sensation may need more visual stimulation in order to attend. They may need colour-coded areas on the table to see where to put their things or benefit from coloured marks at the start of each line to show them where to start writing. Similarly, a child may benefit from sitting facing the front of the class so they are more likely to register when they need to look towards the teacher.

Discuss any planned changes to the layout of the classroom in advance. A child with SPD may notice every change such as wall displays, a shelf that has been tidied, etc., so consider making changes incrementally rather than a large change on the same day. Allow them to help you make the changes and choose where to sit. If you are planning on re-arranging the tables, ask them to help you, and give them a choice of two places. If they feel in control of a change, they are less likely to react adversely to it.

Auditory

Noisy environments (such as a classroom) can be difficult for a child with SPD to tolerate. They may find the noise uncomfortable or painful.

- Within a classroom, be aware of **environmental sounds** (e.g. lights buzzing, door creaking, other children chatting, people walking past outside). If a child has difficulty in following directions, see if there are environmental sounds that may be taking their attention. Carefully choosing the position of the child in the room (or creating quiet work spaces) may benefit both a sensitive child and a child with low registration.
- **Volume control.** Agree with your class hand gestures to ask for an increase or decrease in volume (or use the 'volume control visual' suggested in the Target Ladder on page 53).
- **Breaks.** Some children who are extremely sensitive may need to work outside the class for short periods or wear ear defenders (www.ldalearning.com) during noisy activities or at intervals to give their auditory system a break.
- **Pitch.** Both children who are sensitive and those that have low registration may have difficulties in picking out the teacher's voice from background noise. Make sure you have their attention visually and a quiet classroom before you speak. New sounds are more likely to get all children's attention, so changing the intonation or pitch of your voice for a new instruction will also help the child to register and attend to it.

Tactile

If a child is sensitive to touch, try and position them in a place that minimises other children bumping into them as they are passing.

- **When in line** they may prefer to be at the back or at the front, so they only have one other person beside them.

- **Fidget toy**. If a child likes to touch others or things on the desk, you might allow them to hold something (e.g. a piece of Blu Tack®, a stress ball, or a suitable 'fidget toy' (www.ldalearning.com)) to provide the sensory feedback in a more suitable way.
- **Safe space/quiet spot**. If a child gets overloaded by the various sensory inputs they receive during the day, consider having a quiet space/chill-out zone for the child to access to avoid meltdowns. This could be simply a beanbag on the floor in the carpet area or a pop-up tent with cushions. Regular breaks could be scheduled on the visual timetable. Alternatively, consider a system where the child can let you know if they feel they need a break and be given a break (for an agreed amount of time) in the chill-out space.

Creating an appropriate sensory diet for a child with SPD should be regarded as a 'reasonable adjustment' and not a privilege which can be revoked if the child's behaviour doesn't meet the norms expected.

Taste and smell: lunch/break time issues

Children with SPD can have extremely restricted diets. It is beyond the scope of the class teacher to attempt to tackle these issues singlehandedly within the school day. However, you can support interventions that parents, speech and language therapists and occupational therapists are implementing.

Including education on eating a healthy balanced diet in classroom teaching may encourage healthy eating in some children. Also, a whole-school healthy eating policy where treats (sweets, crisps, cakes, etc.) are not allowed during the school day can also assist in encouraging children to try a wider variety of food.

If a child is trying a new food for the first time, praise them or reward them with stickers. Similarly, praise the child for any attempt to join the group and eat their own food with other children. For example, if the child walks through the dining hall on their way to the playground and has never done this before, reward this effort with praise or a sticker or other suitable reward system.

Don't forget that eating is a multi-sensory experience. It involves not only the taste and smell of the food but also the sound and texture of the food, the way the food looks and how the child's body reacts internally to the food, as well as what is going on in the environment at the time. Hence, consider all other sensory aspects, too, when attempting an intervention to improve eating.

Routine within the classroom

All children benefit from a predictable routine and clear rules. It is easier to follow instructions and class routines when the children know what to expect. Even as adults, we find unexpected changes a little anxiety-provoking. For example, imagine your regular bus route is changed, but you don't know until you are already on the bus. You may feel a little flustered, anxious or annoyed at first. For children this is the same. If the routine or the environment keep changing without prior warning, the child may feel anxious, confused or upset. As we discussed earlier, an increase in emotion can increase sensory sensitivity, so keeping things as stable and predictable as possible is essential for children with SPD.

Using a visual timetable (one picture for each key activity planned for the day) to show children the planned events can be useful to prevent anxiety (Lyon et al, 2014). If, for example, PE time is changed because the hall is in use, then the picture for PE can be moved to later in the day, so the child can still see on the timetable that they will be doing it later.

A child who is very sensitive is likely to perceive every small change, for example, chairs moved, the teacher's clothes, another child absent from the class, etc. Social Stories™ (www.carolgraysocialstories.com) can be used to explain unplanned events or changes in routine, such as school outings or a change in teacher.

Remember that any change (especially if it is unexpected) may make the child more anxious, so they may be more sensitive to sensation and need extra sensory breaks (quiet time, movement, etc.) in order to help process the additional sensory information and avoid sensory overload.

Educating the class about sensory differences

You may consider educating the class more about the senses in order to give the children a vocabulary to discuss their sensory preferences. If the whole class can talk about the sensory experiences they like or don't like, then they may understand why some children need a different routine or particular pieces of specialised equipment. You may discover many of the children have strong dislikes of particular sounds or textures that you weren't aware of. Referring to your own sensory preferences, such as '*I love the taste of broccoli but I don't really like peas*', can also be useful so the child with SPD does not feel singled out or different.

Books and programmes such as *Max and Me: A Story about Sensory Processing* (Lawlor, 2016) and *How Does Your Engine Run?: A Leader's Guide to the Alert Program for Self-Regulation* (Williams & Shellenberger, 1996) provide a vocabulary for teaching the class more about sensory processing if you wish to pursue further training on the subject. For further courses and information on sensory integration issues within the classroom see the Sensory Integration Network (www.sensoryintegration.org.uk).

Not making the child with SPD feel different

Where possible, any accommodations or changes made for the child with SPD in the classroom should be done discreetly. For example, if using a visual timetable or timer, use it for the whole class, and all the children can take turns to put the picture in a 'finished box' when the activity is complete. 'Normalising' sensory likes and dislikes and teaching children about how everyone has individual preferences will help build the child with SPD's self-esteem and confidence.

Sensory overload

Children who are sensitive are more likely to become overloaded or overwhelmed by their environment. This usually presents as a 'meltdown' where the child becomes upset, angry, or anxious. Sensory overload is not the same as a tantrum or behavioural outburst. The child is reacting to their sensory system being saturated by sensory input, and to them the reaction is in proportion to what they are experiencing.

The best way to deal with a meltdown is to try and avoid it by adapting the environment as far as possible to match the child's sensory preferences. However, the child's ability to process sensation fluctuates from day to day depending on various factors, such as how much sleep they have had, their physical health and other stressful life events that they may be experiencing, so sensory overload may be unavoidable at times.

Signs that a child may be becoming over-alerted

Different children show different physical 'signals' when their anxiety and stress levels are rising. As you get to know the child, look for the signs that stress is building so that you can avoid a meltdown. The child can gradually learn to take responsibility for recognising their own physical symptoms. Reflecting what you see can help the child identify and name the physical sensation and request the appropriate strategy to avoid a meltdown. For example, *'Archie, I can see that you are beginning to fidget more and you are breathing more quickly. Would you like to take a short break?'*. Common 'signals' include the following, but this list is not exhaustive.

- Increase in movement/restlessness/fidgeting.
- Increase in repetitive sensory behaviours such as pacing, rocking or hand flapping.
- Increase in breathing rate.
- Perspiration.
- Complaining of nausea or dizziness.
- Increase in vocalisations or asking repetitive questions.
- Covering ears.
- Refusal to comply/participate in an activity.
- Increase in mouthing/chewing of objects.
- Self-injurious behaviour.

Avoiding sensory overload

The following strategies may help prevent sensory overload.

- **Sensory profile**. Get to know the child's sensory profile. Talk to the child's parents and occupational therapist about which of the child's senses are most sensitive.
- **Adapt the classroom**. Try and match the classroom to the child as far as possible. For example, if the child doesn't like being touched/bumped into by others, then seat them with plenty of space around them. Or if a child is very sensitive to noise, create a quiet area in the classroom that they can retreat to if needed.
- **Visual timetable**. If the child can anticipate the sensory experiences that are planned for an activity or day this will reduce anxiety, which in turn will increase their tolerance for sensation.
- **Sensory breaks**. Allow the child to have regular sensory breaks between activities. Depending on the sensory needs of the child, this could consist of a movement break, doing some 'heavy work', body awareness activities or putting on headphones to decrease the auditory input.
- **Don't push the child to finish**. If a child is becoming over-alerted, it is better to allow them to have a break than to press them to continue.
- **Sensory overload**. Teach the child to recognise their own 'signs' of sensory overload. You can do this by reflecting back to the child, for example, *'It seems like the noise is bothering you, would you like to go outside?'*. By giving the child the language to express their sensory overload they may begin to use it themselves. Programmes such as *How Does Your Engine Run?: A Leader's Guide to the Alert Program for Self-Regulation* (Williams & Shellenberger, 1996) or *Max and Me: A Story about Sensory Processing* (Lawlor, 2016) aim to do this too.

If a child has a sensory meltdown

If a child does become upset or distressed due to sensory overload, remember that they are experiencing too much sensory information to process; therefore, it might be useful to:

- keep your own voice low and calm;
- move to a quieter area;
- save any conversations about what happened, or what to do next time, until the child is calm;
- if possible, move outdoors as nature is naturally calming;
- if you have a swing in the playground, allow the child to gently swing themselves backwards and forwards;
- give the child water or something to suck;
- make sure they are not too hot – remove their jumper if appropriate;
- ask them to take some deep breaths;
- do some 'heavy work', such as pushing against the wall, pushing hands together or chair push-ups (Biel, 2009).

The child's reaction is always in proportion to what they are experiencing or perceiving, so it is important that they are not punished for their reaction. However, if they hurt another child or teacher when upset, this can be discussed with them later when they are calm. Teach alternative strategies and use reward systems when they use a more appropriate strategy (such as deep breathing).

Understanding behaviour through the lens of SPD

The school day is a constant barrage of sensory information for all children. Every activity the child is engaged in provides a multi-sensory experience. For example, consider transitioning through the school – the child's visual system has to scan the environment, they may touch other people, there are sounds all around them, perhaps smells as they pass other classrooms, and the child also needs to be aware of their own body position in relation to others. Hence, all the senses play a part in a child completing this activity successfully. For a child with SPD this can be exhausting since their sensory systems can become easily overloaded or fail to register relevant sensory information. Hence, when considering inappropriate/difficult 'behaviours', we must always consider all of the sensory aspects involved from all of the senses and any environmental or activity adaptations that we can make to support the child. It is important to consider the following questions:

- Which senses may be involved in this behaviour/issue?
- Can I provide a sensory strategy to help the child?
- Can I adapt the environment/activity to match the child's sensory needs?
- Are there any other issues going on in the child's life that may be contributing to a difficult behaviour (e.g. bullying/stress at home, illness)?
- Am I communicating clearly with the child so they understand what is expected from them?

It can sometimes be useful to brainstorm all of the factors involved in a particular behaviour. The 'Making changes brainstorming sheet' on page 33 can provide a useful guide to discuss all the issues as a team. (A blank template for photocopying is provided on page 70.)

Making changes brainstorming sheet

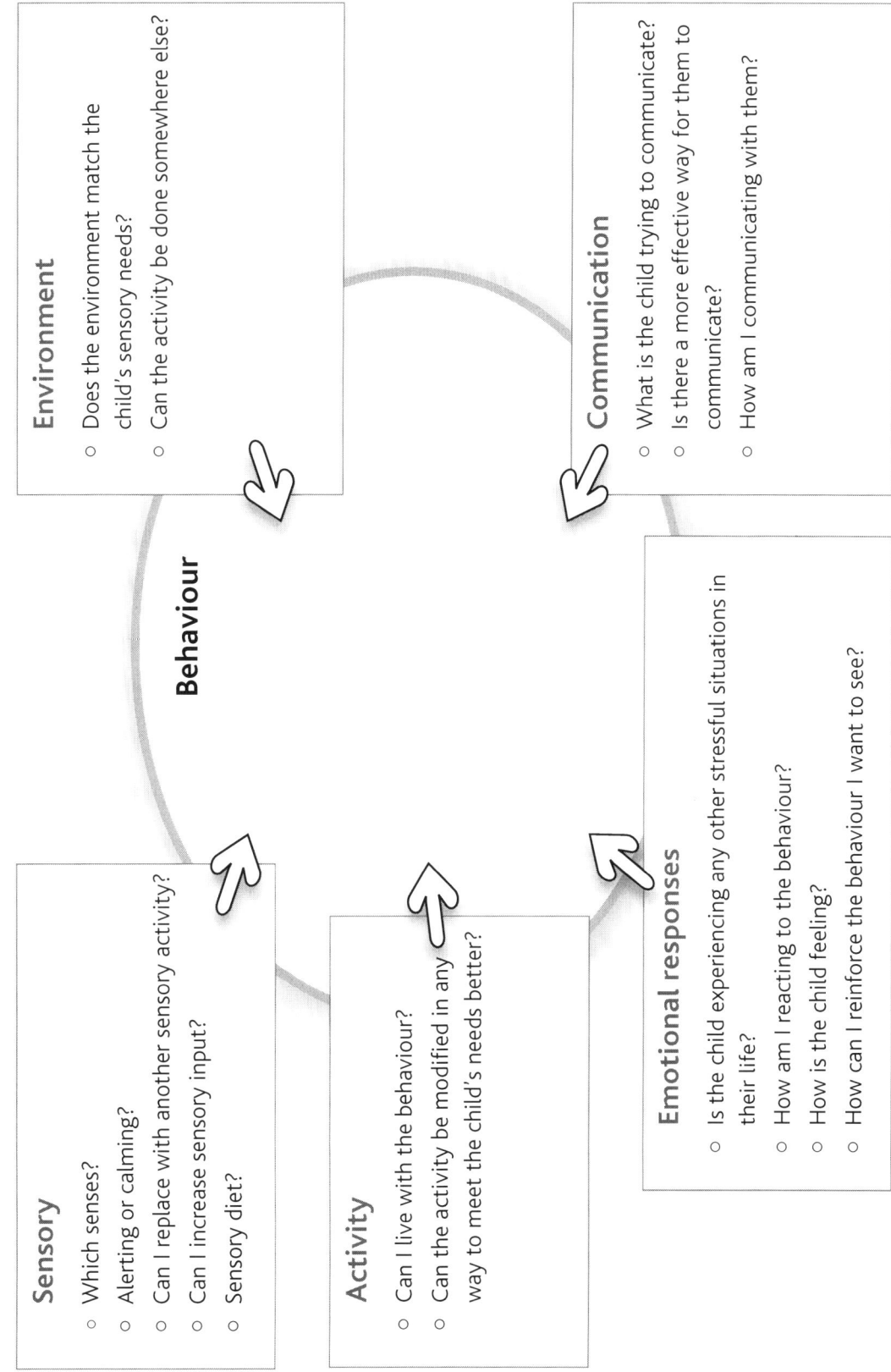

Environment
- Does the environment match the child's sensory needs?
- Can the activity be done somewhere else?

Communication
- What is the child trying to communicate?
- Is there a more effective way for them to communicate?
- How am I communicating with them?

Emotional responses
- Is the child experiencing any other stressful situations in their life?
- How am I reacting to the behaviour?
- How is the child feeling?
- How can I reinforce the behaviour I want to see?

Activity
- Can I live with the behaviour?
- Can the activity be modified in any way to meet the child's needs better?

Sensory
- Which senses?
- Alerting or calming?
- Can I replace with another sensory activity?
- Can I increase sensory input?
- Sensory diet?

Behaviour

Creating a sensory-friendly classroom

Sensory Processing

Dr Ross Greene (author of *The Explosive Child* and *Lost at School*) recommends that when working with children who are hyper-sensitive, we need to start with three assumptions:

1. The child wants to succeed. Children are more motivated by praise and success than by punishment and defeat.
2. If the child lacks the skills to be successful, we need to teach the skills.
3. We need to change the conditions (the environment, our expectations, our responses) before we try to change the child.

These three assumptions mean that we need to change the way we interpret 'inappropriate' behaviour and try to see things from the child's point of view.

Consider, for example, the following 'behaviours'. Understanding them as a mismatch between the child's sensory system and the environment or activity allows us to search for a wider range of solutions.

What we see	What the child may be experiencing	Sensory systems that may be involved
Aggression	Anxiety and confusion	All
Running away	Sensory overload	All
Refusal to comply	Lack of understanding	Auditory
Easily distracted	Inability to know where to focus attention	Auditory, visual
Fidgeting	Difficulty balancing on chair and difficulty in remaining alert	Vestibular, proprioception
Bumping into people and things	Frustration	Visual, vestibular, proprioception
Rough play	Confusion, social isolation	Proprioception, tactile
Inappropriate response to discipline	Communication difficulties	Auditory
Slow to complete work	Lack of clarity, under-responsive sensory system	All
Regular toilet accidents	Embarrassment, lack of awareness	Interoception, tactile

Of course, the cause of these behaviours and experiences will vary from child to child. However, if we always consider behaviours through an 'SPD lens', we have a better chance of working out what the child's difficulties are and then thinking about how to address them.

But remember, in order to achieve successful outcomes for the child, we, the adults, need to support the child to make changes where they don't have the skills to make the changes themselves. The activities in this book are intended to address that skills gap.

How to use this book

You will find a simple four-step summary of how to use this book on page 38.

Every child with SPD has different strengths and weaknesses. The priority for addressing these will be determined by the difficulties currently being faced by the child and will depend on your professional judgement, supported by the child's current anxieties.

To support you with focused target setting, the book is structured as follows:

- Seven different Aspects of sensory processing have been identified (see Fig. 6 on page 36). Think about the child's difficulties: which of these Aspects is causing most concern at the moment?
- Within each Aspect there are three or four different Target Ladders, each based on a particular area of challenge. This is intended to help you to think carefully about precisely where the barrier may be.
- The relevant Target Ladder can then be used to identify the 'next step' target for the child.
- Suggested activities and strategies offer classroom-friendly ideas so you can support the child to meet their target.

For example, as you can see in Fig. 7 on page 37, difficulties with **Aspect 6: Gustatory and olfactory (taste and smell)** can be subdivided into specific areas to work on: tolerating smell, seeking sensation and varying diet. Each Target Ladder contains between 10 and 22 targets.

Aspects, Target Ladders and targets

Aspects

The seven different Aspects identified in this book describe contexts and difficulties which are frequently faced by children who have SPD. In order to identify the most appropriate Aspect for a particular child you will need to consider the most significant barrier for them: for example, if a child has difficulty completing their work, are they having difficulty following verbal instructions in a noisy classroom, or are they having difficulty visually attending to the page?

Sensory Processing

The Aspects of sensory processing identified in this book are:

1. Visual (sight)
2. Auditory (hearing)
3. Tactile (touch)
4. Vestibular (movement and balance)
5. Proprioception (body awareness)
6. Gustatory and olfactory (taste and smell)
7. Interoception (internal body functions and emotions)

Target Ladders

Each of the Aspects is further subdivided into either three or four Target Ladders, each of which addresses different parts of the Aspect. These enable you to develop your understanding of the child's individual needs, 'drilling down' to assist you to identify the child's particular strengths and weaknesses. The Target Ladders are set out on pages 44–69.

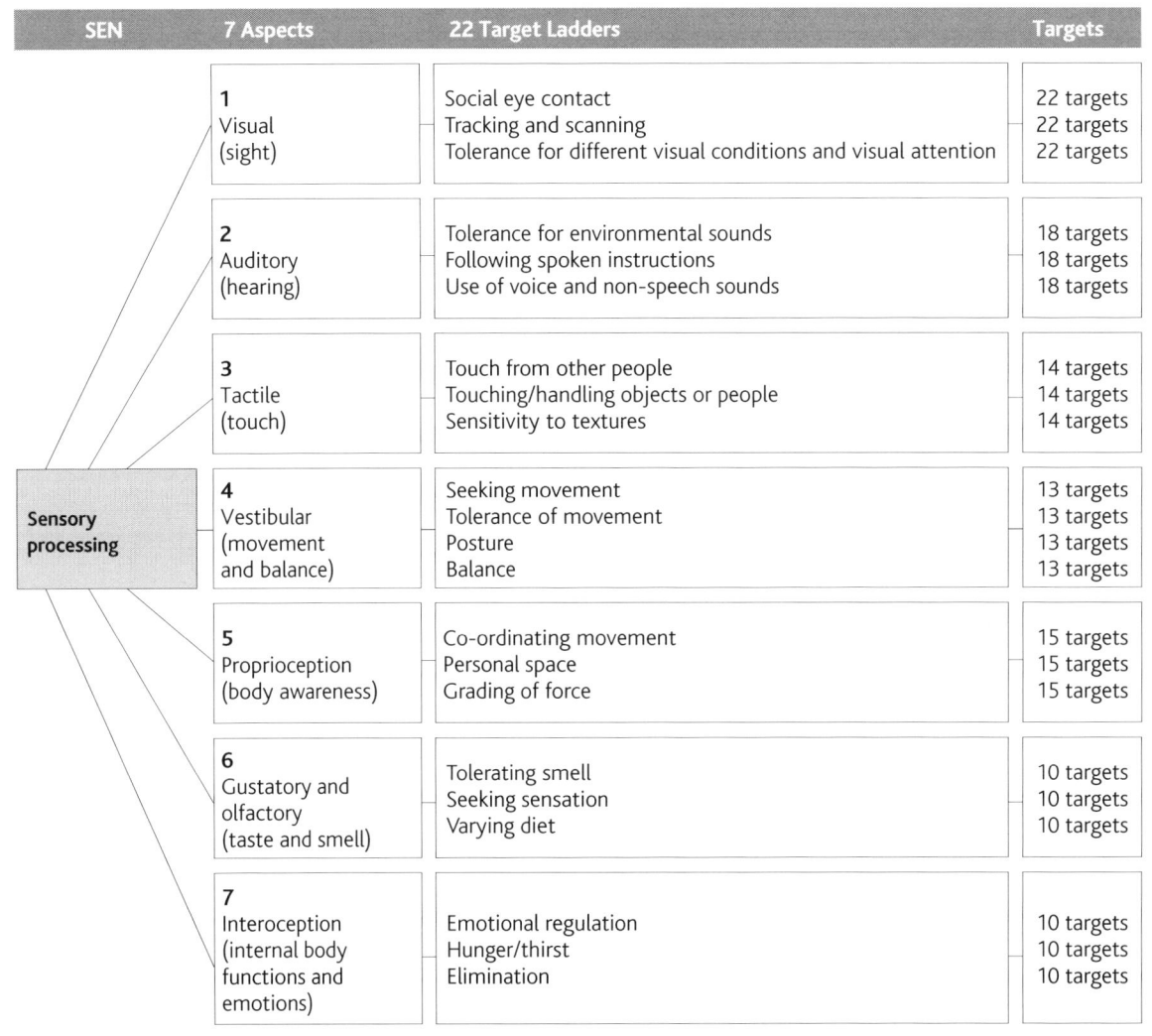

SEN	7 Aspects	22 Target Ladders	Targets
Sensory processing	1 Visual (sight)	Social eye contact Tracking and scanning Tolerance for different visual conditions and visual attention	22 targets 22 targets 22 targets
	2 Auditory (hearing)	Tolerance for environmental sounds Following spoken instructions Use of voice and non-speech sounds	18 targets 18 targets 18 targets
	3 Tactile (touch)	Touch from other people Touching/handling objects or people Sensitivity to textures	14 targets 14 targets 14 targets
	4 Vestibular (movement and balance)	Seeking movement Tolerance of movement Posture Balance	13 targets 13 targets 13 targets 13 targets
	5 Proprioception (body awareness)	Co-ordinating movement Personal space Grading of force	15 targets 15 targets 15 targets
	6 Gustatory and olfactory (taste and smell)	Tolerating smell Seeking sensation Varying diet	10 targets 10 targets 10 targets
	7 Interoception (internal body functions and emotions)	Emotional regulation Hunger/thirst Elimination	10 targets 10 targets 10 targets

Fig. 6: The structure of *Target Ladders: Sensory Processing*.

Targets

There are up to 22 targets in each Target Ladder, with the simplest ones labelled with the letter A, then moving through the alphabet up to N, which are the most difficult. In most of the Target Ladders there are two rows that are labelled with the same letter, because all of the targets in those rows are at a similar developmental level. It is unlikely that any child will need to have all of the targets in each letter band: use your knowledge of the child to identify what they already know and to prioritise what is important.

Letter	Tolerating smell	Seeking sensation	Varying diet
A	With support/accommodation, tolerates day-to-day smells in the classroom	With support and using a suitable chewable toy, attends to class activities with constant use of item in the mouth	With support, eats the same lunch every day in a quiet space away from other children
A	Tolerates day-to-day smells in classroom	With prompting and using a suitable chewable toy, attends to class activities with constant use of item in the mouth	With support, will taste one new food once a week in a quiet space away from other children
A	With support/accommodation, tolerates strong smells around the school	With support and using a suitable chewable toy, attends to class activities with frequent use of item in the mouth	With encouragement, eats the same lunch every day in a quiet space away from other children
A	With support/accommodation, tolerates smells in a quiet space with others eating lunch	With prompting and using a suitable chewable toy, attends to class activities with frequent use of item in the mouth	With support, will try one new food each day in a quiet space away from other children

Fig. 7: Part of the Target Ladders table for **Aspect 6: Gustatory and olfactory (taste and smell)** showing how targets are structured in the Ladders.

Although within each Target Ladder rows with the same letter are similar, this is not the case between the different Target Ladders. So a child may have an A target in one Ladder and a G target in another. Some of the Target Ladders start at a very early developmental level, whereas others assume a level of competence even in the A rows. Again, use your professional judgement, and be guided by the child's abilities and needs. The letters are simply there to help you to identify targets which are at approximately the same developmental level within the same Target Ladder.

The targets are all written in positive language. This is to support you when you look through them to find out what the child *can already* do. Use them as the basis of the target you set for the child.

As you track the statements through each Ladder identifying what the child can already do, be aware of missed steps. If a child has missed one of the steps, further progress up that Ladder may be insecure. Many children learn to mask the missed step, using developing skills in other areas to help them, but the time may come when the missed step will cause difficulties.

Activities and strategies to achieve the targets

In the Target Ladders on pages 44–69, targets are listed on left-hand pages. The corresponding right-hand pages offer ideas for activities or strategies that you might use to help to achieve the targets. These are suggestions only – but many have been used successfully in classrooms and are accepted good practice. The activities or strategies are shown at the point in the developmental process at which they are likely to make the most impact.

The suggested activities can often be adapted to work for a range of targets within this stage of the Ladder. For this reason, activities are generally not linked to individual targets.

How to set targets: a four-step summary

1. **Use Fig. 6 on page 36 to identify the one or two Aspects of sensory processing that are most challenging for the child.** Please use the checklist on pages 22–23 for guidance.

2. **Use the Target Ladders tables on pages 44–69** to pinpoint specific targets for the child to work towards. Look at easier targets in the same Ladder to ensure that the child has achieved all of those.

3. **Photocopy the relevant targets page** so that you can:
   - highlight and date those the child can already do;
   - identify the next priorities.

4. **Use the Record of Progress sheet on page 41 to create a copy of the targets for the child or their parents.**

Making the most of Target Ladders

You may find the following tips helpful when setting your targets.

- Talk to the child about what they would like to improve; a target that the child wants to improve is more likely to be successful.
- Discuss targets with the child's parents/carers.
- Think about your main concerns about that child's learning.
- Once you have identified the Aspect, identify the most beneficial Target Ladder.
   - Look for any 'missed steps', and target those first. The child is likely to find success fairly quickly and will be motivated to continue to try to reach new targets.
   - Talk to the child and agree an appropriate target based on your skills inventory. Again, targets which the child is aware of tend to be achieved most quickly and are motivational.
- The target does not have to be the lowest unachieved statement in any Ladder: use your professional judgement and knowledge of the child to identify the most useful and important target for the child.

- No child will follow all of the targets in precisely the order listed. Use your professional judgement, and your knowledge about what the child can already do, to identify the most appropriate target and be realistic in your expectations. There may be some zigzagging up and down a Target Ladder.
- When setting targets, always ask yourself practical questions:
  - What can I put in place in order to enable the child to meet the targets?
  - Which people and resources are available to support the child?
  - What is the likelihood of a child achieving a target within the next half-term?
  - Which targets have been agreed with other children in the class?

It is important that the targets you set are realistic considering the time, the adult support and the resources available.

Once you have identified what the child can already achieve, continue to highlight and update the sheets each time the child achieves a new target. Celebrate progress with the child while, at the same time, constantly checking to ensure that previously achieved targets remain secure. If any target becomes insecure, revisit it briefly, without setting a formal target, in order to give the child an opportunity to consolidate the skill without feeling that they are going backwards in their achievements.

Records of Progress

Creating a Record of Progress

If the child can communicate confidently, arrange to meet with them and their parents and ask them first to tell you what they are good at. When working with the child, you may need to adapt the immediate visual environment to support them. For example, any task sheet may need to be simplified and/or enlarged. You may wish to colour-code the chart, or consider carefully the colour of paper and text or the style of font. Record their responses on the Record of Progress (RoP). A blank form is supplied for you to copy on page 41. Ask the child and their parents then to tell you which areas they would most like to improve.

If your school operates a Pupil Passport system, then you may want to amend the RoP form, but you will nonetheless need a sheet that can be annotated and amended.

As you add one or two more targets, talk to the child and their parents to check that they agree that each target is relevant and that they understand what they will need to do to achieve their targets. Targets that children do not know or care about are much harder for them to achieve. Limit the number of targets to a maximum of three. Remember, you do not need to use the precise wording of the targets given in this book: adapt the words to match the maturity and understanding of the learner. Monitor the impact of any intervention (see page 42) and review at regular intervals – at least half-termly – to see if there is an impact. If not, consider whether a different intervention would be more effective.

Principles for the effective use of an RoP include the following:

- The form must be 'live'. The child will need to have access to it at all times, as will all adults who work with the child, in order that it can be referred to, amended and updated regularly. Ensure that the child's parents/carers have a copy. If you think that the child is likely to lose or destroy their RoP, make a photocopy so that you can supply another.
- Together with the child, you have identified their priority areas to focus on. Management and support for these should be consistent across the school day and from all adults.
- As soon as each target has been achieved, according to the success criteria you agreed, the form should be dated and a 'next step' considered.
- When you set up the RoP, agree a review date which is ideally about half a term ahead and no more than one term ahead. Do not wait until this date to identify that targets have been achieved, but on this date review progress towards all targets – or identified next steps – and agree new targets.
- If a target has not been achieved, consider why not. If possible, try a different approach to meeting the target. Having the same target over and over is likely to bore the child and put them off following their RoP.

RECORD OF PROGRESS

Name _____ Class _____ Date agreed _____ RoP number: _____

Review date _____

My targets are	I will know that I have achieved my target when I can	Date when I achieved my target	Next steps
I am good at			
I would like to be better at			
It helps me when			

Targets approved by: Pupil _____ Teacher _____

SENCO _____ Parent/Carer _____

© Inés Lawlor 2017 *Target Ladders: Sensory Processing* LDA Permission to photocopy

Monitoring a Record of Progress

In order to ensure that your Record of Progress (RoP) is used effectively, you need to monitor progress towards the targets each time you offer support. Use a monitoring sheet; a photocopiable example is given on page 43.

- Use a separate sheet – copied on to a different colour of paper – for each target.
- Write the child's name at the top of the sheet and the target underneath.
- On each occasion when someone works with the child towards the target, they should write the smaller, more specific target that they are working towards *during this session* in the Target box.
- They should then write a comment. On each occasion the child achieves the target during the session and then back in class, tick the box.

The intention is that these sheets should be used to create a cumulative record of a child's progress towards their target. The evidence here can be used to assess the impact of an intervention in order that its appropriateness can be evaluated swiftly and any additional actions can be taken promptly.

What precisely you record will depend on the type of support being offered and the nature of the target.

- If you are delivering a planned intervention, make a record of the unit/page/activity and a comment about the learning the child demonstrated. For example, a comment relating to a target about the child's balance may be: *'Was able to balance when running in a straight line during 'What's the time Mr Wolf?' but required assistance during tag when running in all directions.'*
- If you are offering support in the classroom, you might want to comment on the child's learning over a few lessons. Focus on what the child has achieved in the lessons and whether the learning is secure.
- As a general principle, aim to include more positive than negative comments, and always try to balance a negative with a positive comment.

At the half-termly review of the RoP, collect together all of the monitoring sheets and look at the frequency of the comments against each target as well as the learning they reflect. If a child has had absences, or an intervention has not happened as often as planned, consider what impact that has had on the effectiveness of the intervention. If the intervention has gone as planned, look at the progress charted and ask yourself these questions:

- Is it swift enough? Is the intervention helping this child to close the gap? Is the adult working with the child the best person for the job?
- Is this the best intervention? Is there anything else you can reasonably do in school?
- What should happen next? If the intervention was successful, do you continue it, develop it, consolidate it or change to a different target?

At the end of the process, create a new RoP with the child and their parents/carers and use a new monitoring sheet.

Monitoring the progress of _____ towards meeting the target of _____

Date	Today's Target	Comment	Achieved			

The Target Ladders

Aspect 1: Visual (sight)

Letter	Social eye contact	Tracking and scanning	Tolerance for different visual conditions and visual attention
A	When one-to-one with a familiar person, occasionally makes eye contact for 1–2 seconds	Momentarily focuses on a familiar object held in their line of vision	With support, tolerates a familiar environment (e.g. a quiet space outside the classroom near a window)
A	When one-to-one with a familiar person, makes eye contact when prompted for 1–2 seconds	When prompted, tracks an object from either left or right to the midline moving head and eyes together	With prior warning, tolerates small changes in the environment
B	When one-to-one with a familiar person, makes eye contact for 3–4 seconds at regular intervals	Notices and looks down at an object that is placed on a table in front of them when sitting	Tolerates a familiar uncluttered space with natural lighting
B	When one-to-one with an unfamiliar adult, makes eye contact for 1–2 seconds when prompted	Tracks an object from either left or right to the midline with eyes only	Maintains interest in one object for 3–4 seconds when the environment remains the same
C	When one-to-one with an unfamiliar person, occasionally makes eye contact for 1–2 seconds	Tracks an object from left to right (or right to left) crossing the midline with eyes only	Maintains interest in one object for up to 30 seconds in a busy environment
D	Uses eye contact with a familiar person with a social reaction (e.g. smiling or waving goodbye)	Notices and attempts to pick up an object that is placed on a table in front of them	With prompting, brings attention back to an object placed in front of them
E	During a familiar routine or activity, looks at the person when prompted (e.g. when their name is called on the register)	Notices and is able to pick up a small object that is placed on a table in front of them with accuracy	With prompting and assistance, moves between environments with changing lighting conditions
F	With prompting, stops the activity they are doing and looks to greet someone familiar when they enter the room	Tracks a moving object/person in all directions	With prior notice, tolerates other children moving position in the room

Suggested activities or strategies

Social eye contact

Looking at someone's face, particularly giving eye contact, can be very difficult for children with SPD as the changing nature of facial expressions and movement of the eyes can be difficult for them to process. It is therefore important not to force eye contact if the child finds it distressing. However, you can encourage eye contact through the following strategies:

- **Change your intonation and tone.** Try a more animated tone to bring the child's attention to you. The child's sensory system will naturally respond to new or interesting sights. A cue such as a soft sounding chime or bell may help the child recognise when it is time to look at you.
- **Use a song to prompt.** Encourage the child to look at you to say hello by singing a hello song (e.g. *'We'll say hello to John, we'll say hello to John, we're glad you came today, we'll say hello to John'* or *'Where is Michael, where is Michael? There he is, there he is. He's come to play today, he's come to play today and he's looking at me, looking at me'*).
- **Role-play with puppets.** Use puppets to 'act out' a social interaction (e.g. saying hello to your teacher). Make sure the child knows social vocabulary for the situation (e.g. *'Hello, how are you?'*). Ask them to use their character to greet your character. Model an appropriate response both in words and in gaze. Explicitly point out that your character is looking at, and making brief eye contact with, the child's character. Swap roles. Check that the child's character responds to yours in an appropriate way.
- **Role-play.** Repeat the role-play activity above without puppets. First, allow the child to come into a space and call your name. Make appropriate responses. Then swap roles. Praise the child for making eye contact when responding to, or making, a greeting.

Tracking and scanning

A child with SPD may find attending to their work on the page difficult. This may be due to distractions in the classroom or on the table, or a difficulty with focusing on only one part of the page at a time. The following strategies may help build up the child's ability to track and scan:

- **Focus.** Encourage the child to focus on an object in front of them by playing with toys and games at a tabletop.
- **Attention.** Using an object that is of interest to the child (e.g. a pencil with a toy/figure on the end), play a game where they have to keep their eyes on the figure at all times and try to stop them from getting 'lost'. If they lose their attention visually, say *'Oops, you've lost him'* and bring the object back to their line of vision.
- **Tracking.** Move a pencil/object slowly to the level of the nose. Then ask the child to follow the pencil as you move it: up and down in a vertical line, side to side at eye level, diagonally from top right corner to bottom left and top left to bottom right and vice versa, then from far away to near so the eyes converge.
- **Scanning.** Ball games encourage the two eyes to work together. Start sitting across the table from each other or on the floor 1m apart. Roll a ball backwards and forwards, gradually increase the distance and encourage the child to watch the ball all the way. Alternatively, use a target such as 'skittles'.

Tolerance for different visual conditions and visual attention

- **Keep lighting natural where possible.** Natural lighting is more calming, so if possible allow the child to sit near a window. If the room is too bright for the child, consider installing blinds.
- **Allow more time to adjust.** Be aware that it can take the child a while to adjust when moving through the school with various lighting conditions, and take this into account when beginning a new activity.
- **Wear sunglasses outside on a bright day.** You may ask the parents to send the child to school with sunglasses or a sun hat and wear them at home.

Aspect 1: Visual (sight)

Letter	Social eye contact	Tracking and scanning	Tolerance for different visual conditions and visual attention
G	Without prompting, stops the activity they are doing and looks to greet someone unfamiliar	Moves towards moving object and attempts to catch/grab it	Tolerates other children moving position in the room (without prior notice) whilst remaining in the same place themselves
H	Sometimes makes eye contact when talking themselves	With assistance, locates own seat in the classroom and moves towards it	At a table with prompting and support, sustains attention for a preferred fine motor task (e.g. building blocks or a jigsaw)
H	Looks in the general direction of the person speaking when in a group	Locates and moves towards own seat without bumping into others	With prior notice, tolerates multiple changes in classroom layout
I	Consistently uses eye contact when talking themselves	Locates items on a table	Without prompting, sustains visual attention on a preferred task or game at a table in order to complete the task
J	Sometimes uses eye contact to indicate listening at the start of an interaction	With support, copies one letter at a time from a card placed in front of them on a table	With support, can tolerate environments where other children are moving (e.g. the playground)
J	Looks at the person speaking when in a group	When reading with assistance, tracks each letter left to right across a page	With one-to-one assistance within the classroom, completes half of given classwork within the allocated time
K	Uses eye contact intermittently during a short conversation (1–2 minutes)	With support, copies one word at a time from a card placed in front of them	When standing still, tolerates environments where other children are moving (e.g. PE or the playground)
K	Uses eye contact to indicate listening at the start of an interaction	When reading with assistance, tracks each word from left to right	With one-to-one assistance within the classroom, completes given classwork within the allocated time

Suggested activities or strategies

Social eye contact

- Praise when they get it right. Use phrases like *'Thanks for looking at me when I called your name'*, *'Great looking at Adam when you were playing'*. This will reinforce appropriate eye contact.
- If the child finds eye contact difficult during play, try setting up activities where eye contact isn't as necessary. For example, if two children are sharing construction or creative resources, they would generally look towards the activity. However, the children can still interact through conversation and sharing ideas without engaging in regular eye contact with each other, especially if they are sitting side by side rather than facing each other. The child with SPD will be more relaxed this way, and eye contact may occur naturally.
- Teach the child other strategies to interact with another person without looking directly at them, by shifting the focus onto a shared object or encouraging them to look near, but not at, the other person's eyes.

Tracking and scanning

Tracking skills can be developed by playing ball games. Encouraging ball games through PE and playground games will help develop smooth co-ordinated use of the eyes.

- Begin with a balloon, scarf or cuddly toy as they move more slowly.
- Practise throwing and catching to each other and throwing into a stationary target. Gradually increase the distance from the target.
- Start with a large ball then try a smaller ball such as a tennis ball.
- Once the child has mastered throwing and catching when looking forwards, ask them to throw the ball up in the air.
- Try and clap before catching the ball. Move on to bouncing it to the ground and catching it. Finally, ask the child to run and catch at the same time (e.g. they have to run towards an x marked on the spot and catch the ball as it's thrown).

Tracking skills can also be developed when reading and writing.

- A slanted work surface for writing reduces the amount of movement of the head and eyes when a child is copying down something from the board. Some children may find it easier to focus their eyes when at an angle rather than completely flat (as this involves more movement of the head). A lever arch folder can be used, or angled writing boards which have a lip to prevent the page slipping can be purchased (www.ldalearning.com).
- It may be useful to block out parts of the worksheet or page that the child is not using. If the child is reading, try using a reading window (www.ldalearning.com). It may make it easier for the child to remain focused on the task.
- For tracking across a page, use your finger or a piece of card with an arrow pointed up at the word the child has to read.

Tolerance for different visual conditions and visual attention

- **Attention.** Praise the child when they look at the place on the page to which you are pointing.
- **Use different coloured paper and pencils.** Some children find coloured paper such as yellow or green with a black pen or white writing on a black background easier to tolerate visually.
- **Rewards and praise.** Have a system for rewarding good attention (e.g. stickers).
- **Timer.** Some children may work better when they know they only have a limited time to complete a task. Ensure the time you allow is appropriate for the child's abilities. An electronic or sand timer that doesn't have a loud bell may be more suitable for children who may have sensitivity to noise.
- **Visual timetables.** Visual timetables can help the child stay on task and motivate them to finish work if they are looking forward to the next activity. Use a 'finished box' to put in the cards for activities that the child has completed to motivate and offer another opportunity for a movement break.

Aspect 1: Visual (sight)

Aspect 1: Visual (sight)

Letter	Social eye contact	Tracking and scanning	Tolerance for different visual conditions and visual attention
L	With support, uses eye contact intermittently when talking with peers in a group	Copies a sentence from a card placed in front of them	With frequent direct support, completes half of given classwork within the allocated time
L	With prompting, maintains appropriate eye contact with an adult when talking and listening for a short conversation (1–2 minutes)	With assistance, copies one or two words from the board	With frequent direct support, completes given work within the allocated time
M	With support, maintains appropriate eye contact when talking with peers in a group	Copies one word from the board	With occasional prompting, completes given work within the allocated time
M	With prompting, maintains appropriate eye contact with an adult when talking and listening for a short conversation (1–2 minutes)	Copies more than one word from the board	Moves (e.g. running, jumping) whilst other children are also moving
N	Without prompting, maintains appropriate eye contact with an adult when talking and listening for a short conversation (1–2 minutes)	Copies short sentences from the board	Without prompting, completes given work within the allocated time
N	Without support, maintains appropriate eye contact when talking with peers in a group	Accurately copies information down from the board	Moves easily between different environments with different lighting conditions (e.g. daylight to darker corridor)

Suggested activities or strategies

Social eye contact

- Use Social Stories™ (www.carolgraysocialstories.com) or Comic Strip Conversations™ (www.carolgraysocialstories.com). These are individualised scenarios where the child can see step-by-step what is expected in a particular situation.
- Use **role-play** to help the child practise scenarios (e.g. asking a friend about their weekend). Teach the child step-by-step how to look at the person when asking a question and when listening. Practise the scenario with each other and then with another child.
- During PE, ask the children to stand in a circle with a soft ball. Each child has to call another child's name, look at them and throw the ball to them.
- During group discussions in the classroom, use an object (e.g. a small ball or a cuddly toy) to indicate whose turn it is to talk. Prompt children to look towards the person who is speaking.
- Talk to the child in private about setting a goal of eye contact and why it is important to others that the child looks at them. Give discreet rewards/praise such as a smiley face on their page or a sticker within the class when the child gets it right.

Tracking and scanning

A child with difficulty in tracking or scanning the environment may have difficulty with finding objects on their table, negotiating the environment, ball skills or poor tolerance of movement.

- **Position in the room.** Ensure the child is sitting so they are facing you, so they do not need to turn their head to see you as this involves more movement of the eyes. If they have difficulty in locating their seat or moving through the class without bumping into others, ensure their chair is positioned in a place with a clear route from the door.
- **Visual scanning.** Activities such as *Where's Wally?* books (Martin Handford, Walker Books), word searches or mazes help the child's visual scanning skills. These could be scanned up on to the board and done as a class.
- **Spell it.** Draw all the letters of the alphabet on a page in a random order. The child uses a straw to blow a small piece of cotton wool to each letter to spell words. This could be used as part of a game of hangman or a way to learn spellings.
- **Board games.** Draughts, chess or Connect Four® where the child has to scan the board to assess where to make the next move improve scanning skills.
- **Card games.** Any card game develops visual scanning skills. Play Happy Families using a standard pack of cards and two players. Each player has four cards each, and four cards are placed face up in a row and the rest of the deck face down. The players race to be the first to collect four cards of the same number by swapping one of their cards for one of the cards in the centre four. Once each player has finished exchanging with the four cards that are in the centre, the cards are placed at the bottom of the deck, and four new cards are placed in the centre. The winner is the first with four cards of the same number.

Tolerance for different visual conditions and visual attention

- **Cover.** When the child is writing or completing a worksheet, try using another page to cover the sections that have already been completed as they move down the page.
- **Movement breaks.** Remember that focusing and staying attentive may be difficult and tiring for the child. Set short tasks that they can achieve and allow regular movement breaks such as allowing the child to bring up their work to you when they are finished, hand out books, sharpen pencils when needed or run errands between classrooms.
- **Playground spaces.** If the child finds tolerating movement or being in spaces where other people are moving difficult, you may want to create different zones for playing in the playground, so one part is for quiet play and another for running. Perhaps a corner of the playground could have a bench for chatting to friends.

Aspect 2: Auditory (hearing)

Letter	Tolerance for environmental sounds	Following spoken instructions	Use of voice and non-speech sounds
A	Registers a new unexpected sound with a startle reaction	Registers and turns to look at a new sound (e.g. a person speaking or entering the room)	Uses voice to get attention
A	Registers a new unexpected sound by covering ears	Registers and turns towards a familiar person when they speak in a quiet environment	With support, waits to speak whilst somebody else is talking one-to-one
B	With support/ears covered, tolerates average classroom noise	Turns towards speaker when name is called in a quiet environment	Uses voice to get another person's attention
B	With support/ears covered, tolerates average playground noise	With support, follows one-step instructions to complete routine activities in a quiet environment	With support, waits to speak whilst somebody else is talking in a group discussion
C	Tolerates average classroom noise	Responds to playground whistle/bell appropriately	Uses voice to get a specific adult's attention
C	Tolerates average playground noise	With support, follows one-step instructions to complete routine activities in the classroom	Waits to speak whilst somebody else is talking in most situations
D	With support/ears covered, tolerates a noisy environment (e.g. assembly, PE)	Turns towards speaker when name is called in a noisy environment	With support, recognises the difference between a quiet voice/non-speech sound and a loud voice/non-speech sound
D	Tolerates a noisy environment (e.g. assembly, PE)	With support, follows one-step instructions to complete routine activities in a noisy environment	Makes a loud voice and non-speech sound

Suggested activities or strategies

Tolerance for environmental sounds

- **Preparing the child for sounds.** If a child anticipates a sound, they are less likely to overperceive its intensity. For example, if a fire alarm is planned, use a Social Story™ and visual timetable to prepare the child for the sound.
- **Ear protectors.** Allowing the child to cover their ears, either with their hands or with sound-blocking headphones (www.ldalearning.com), can provide the child with a sensory break and prevent them becoming overloaded. This can be particularly useful if the child needs to concentrate on a piece of work.
- **Listen to your breathing.** Teach the child to tune in to the sound of their breathing. This can be used when the child is becoming overwhelmed by a sound/an environment. Practise at a calm time in a quiet environment to help the child master the skill first.
  - Ask them to sit in a comfortable position, feet flat on the ground, eyes closed and hands resting on their tummy.
  - Ask the child to close their eyes and breathe normally.
  - If they begin to breathe too quickly, emphasise taking slow deep breaths and feeling the hands move as the tummy rises and falls.
  - Ask them to begin counting their breaths in their head.
  - If they find it difficult, you can help them by counting out loud
  - Once they reach 10, begin from one again.
  - Build the time up to one minute.

Following spoken instructions

- **Visual prompts.** Using pictures (on a visual timetable) and gestures when speaking can help support what you are saying. Show the picture as you give the instruction.
- **Position in the room.** Consider the child's position in the room. If they can see you clearly, they are more likely to pick up signals that you are talking.
- **Listening ears.** Prompt the child to listen by giving an instruction such as *'Turn on your listening ears'*, then ask them to rub their hands and place them to create 'cups' behind their ears.
- **Use clear concise language.** If the child has difficulty following instructions, keep language to short simple sentences. Say *'Put your book away please'*, rather than *'Now children, in a few moments we're going to break, so can you please start to put your books away please'*.
- **Simon Says.** Play games that involve following directions, such as Simon Says. Begin by demonstrating the moves as you say them then build towards instructions only.
- **Following instructions.** Ask the child to stand next to their chair with a pencil. Ask them to put the pencil on, under, in front, behind, on the backrest, go in a circle around the chair.

Use of voice and non-speech sounds

- **Non-speech sounds.** If the child makes non-speech sounds such as humming, singing, shouting during classroom activities, other children may find it disruptive. If other children don't seem to notice and can continue working, then there may be no need to point it out to the child. Try using a social story to explain why it is not appropriate in the class, but it is OK in the playground.
- **Pass a sound.** Decide on an order in which a sound is going to be passed around the class. The children close their eyes and pass a sound around (such as *mmmm*). Only one child makes the sound at a time and can only start making the sound when the last child has finished. This could be linked to the sounds of letters.
- **Guess the emotion.** Choose a sentence (e.g. *How are you today?*) and then say it in different voices. The children have to guess how you are feeling (e.g. excited, sad or worried).
- **Understanding volume.** Develop hand signals to show 'making the sound quieter' and 'making the sound louder'. Use the hand signals throughout the school day.

Aspect 2: Auditory (hearing)

Aspect 2: Auditory (hearing)

Letter	Tolerance for environmental sounds	Following spoken instructions	Use of voice and non-speech sounds
E	With support/ears covered, tolerates a busy and noisy environment (e.g. the dining hall)	With support, follows one-step non-routine/new instructions	Understands the difference between making a loud sound and making a quiet one
E	With prior warning, tolerates familiar loud sounds (e.g. the school bell)	With support, follows two-step instructions (e.g. 'Put your pencil down and close your book')	With support, decreases volume of voice and non-speech sounds
F	Tolerates a busy and noisy environment (e.g. the dining hall)	Follows one-step instructions (e.g. 'Sit down') in a quiet environment	With support, understands when it is appropriate to make non-speech sounds
F	Tolerates familiar loud sounds (e.g. the school bell, the hand dryer)	Follows two-step instructions (e.g. 'Put your pencil down and close your book') in a classroom environment	With prompting, regulates volume of voice between 'indoor voice' and 'outdoor voice'
G	With support, completes tasks in a quiet environment	With support, follows a conversation within a small group in a quiet environment	With support, changes tone of voice to express emotion (e.g. excitement)
G	With support, plays/engages in group activities in a quiet environment	Follows three-step instructions in a quiet environment	Understands when it is appropriate to make non-speech sounds
H	Works independently and completes tasks in a quiet environment	Follows a conversation between a group of children in a quiet environment	Regulates volume of voice between 'indoor voice' and 'outdoor voice'
H	With support, plays/engages in group activities in a noisy environment (e.g. the school hall, the playground)	With support, follows a conversation in a noisy environment	Only makes non-speech sounds (e.g. humming) when appropriate (e.g. at break times)
I	Works independently and completes tasks in a noisy environment	Follows three-step instructions in a noisy environment	Changes tone of voice to express emotions (e.g. excitement)
I	Tolerates unexpected loud sounds (e.g. the fire alarm)	Follows instructions in all environments	Uses appropriate volume of voice for the setting

Suggested activities or strategies

Tolerance for environmental sounds

- **Change routine to minimise exposure to loud sounds.** If a particularly noisy part of the school (e.g. the playground or dining hall) causes distress for the child, consider allowing the child to leave the environment when it is becoming too much, or avoid the environment altogether, and gradually re-introduce the child as his/her tolerance increases. If the child feels they can control how long they spend in the environment, they will be more relaxed overall and can gradually increase their tolerance.
- Wearing ear protectors in noisy environments may help (e.g. the school toilet where hand dryers make sudden, loud noise).

Following spoken instructions

- **Listening games.** Play games to develop listening skills, such as 'whispers' (children are seated in a row and a message is passed in a whisper from one child to the next) or Simon Says. For more listening games try Sensory Shuffle (www.ldalearning.com).
- **Teacher's voice.** If a child is overwhelmed or upset, keep your voice low and calm when talking to them. If a child needs more sensory input in order to attend, you may need to alter the pitch and tone of your voice frequently to get their attention.
- **Focus.** Children with SPD find it difficult to prioritise sensory information they receive, so may focus on a different part of an image to the one you're talking about or to the sound of another child's breathing, rather than to your voice.
  - Before they begin a task, ensure that the child is clear exactly what you need them to achieve. If they can read, give them written success criteria, if not, use pictures.
  - Break the task into small chunks so the child has a reason to move before starting on the next bit.

Use of voice and non-speech sounds

- **Prompting.** You can prompt the child by saying 'indoor voice' or 'outdoor voice' when needed. Social Stories™ can help explain to the child why using different volumes in different situations is necessary.
- **Use a 'talking toy' or 'talking hat'.** When having group discussion within the class, children can be shown how to take turns to talk by putting up their hand and holding an object (e.g. a cuddly toy) when they talk and then passing it to the next child for their turn.
- **Role-play.** Being able to recognise and use different tones of voice to convey different emotions can be difficult for children with SPD. Use role-play and pictures to illustrate this. Choose a line to practise, such as '*Can you all sit down?*', then say it with different tones of voice and the child has to guess whether you are annoyed, happy, sad, worried, etc. by your tone of voice. Make it more difficult by asking the child to close their eyes so they can't read your facial expression.
- **Volume control.** Rating the volume of the voice on a scale or dial (e.g. numbers 1–5 with an arrow that can be moved to point to the number) might help the child to regulate the volume of their voice.
- **Volume visual.** Make a simple volume control visual.
  - Talk to the class about where on the visual their voices should be for different activities.
  - Model using the visual to either congratulate children whose voices are at the right volume or to ask them to reduce the volume.
  - Make an individual copy of the volume control visual for the children with auditory difficulties, so you can discreetly indicate the volume of their voice now and where you would like it to be.
- **Loud and quiet.** Play music quietly then vary the volume. The children have to match the volume of their actions to the volume of the music (e.g. by clicking fingers, clapping with their hands and stamping their feet).

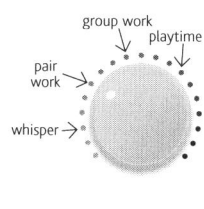

Aspect 3: Tactile (touch)

Letter	Touch from other people	Touching/handling objects or people	Sensitivity to textures
A	Tolerates firm touch from a familiar person (e.g. a hug from a parent)	With support, only touches others in close proximity to them when appropriate	With support, touches dry textures (e.g. playdough) with part of hand
A	Tolerates light predictable touch from a familiar person (e.g. a kiss on the cheek from a parent)	With support, transitions from one place to another without touching others or objects	With support, touches dry textures (e.g. playdough) with whole hand
B	With support, tolerates predictable, brief touch from an unfamiliar adult (e.g. a 'high five')	With prompting, touches others in close proximity to them only when appropriate	With support, touches wet textures (e.g. paints) with fingers
B	With support, tolerates predictable, firm touch from an unfamiliar adult (e.g. shaking their hand)	With prompting, transitions from one place to another without touching others or objects	With support, touches wet textures (e.g. paints) with whole hand
C	Tolerates an unexpected physical prompt from the teacher (e.g. tap on the shoulder)	Touches others in close proximity to them only when appropriate	Tolerates adapted uniform (e.g. no jumper/no tie)
C	Shakes or hold hands with another child or teacher when appropriate	Transitions from one place to another without touching others (other than accidentally)	Touches dry textures (e.g. sand)
D	Tolerates touch when part of a game (e.g. tag, duck duck goose)	Touches others only when appropriate	Touches wet textures (e.g. paint)
D	Tolerates predictable touch for 1–2 minutes (e.g. placing hands on the child in front's shoulders)	Transitions from one place to another without touching others or objects	Tolerates full school uniform

Suggested activities or strategies

Touch from other people

- **Deep pressure touch.** Usually deep, predictable touch is less alerting than light, unexpected touch. If you need to touch the child to get their attention, use a firm touch and forewarn them verbally too. Some children use weighted or deep pressure lap pads or blankets to provide additional deep pressure input. Talk to the child's occupational therapist about whether this may be appropriate.
- **Minimise unexpected touch.** Position the child in the class so other children do not need to brush past them in order to get to their place. When moving from the class to the playground the child might prefer being at the back or front of the line, rather than in the middle. At busy times, such as home time, when lots of classes may be moving through the corridors, consider allowing the child to wait until last, or leave a few minutes early to avoid any accidental pushing/bumping from other children.

Touching/handling objects or people

- Use verbal cues such as '*Say hello to Gemma*' and prompt the child to shake hands with 'Gemma' to illustrate appropriate touch.
- Give the child something else to hold. If the child finds it difficult to sit still or transition without touching objects or other people, give them an object to hold (e.g. a stress ball or a piece of Blu Tack® or a heavy or weighted toy – see www.ldalearning.com).
- **Transitional object.** If a child needs to get more tactile input whilst transitioning from one part of the school to another, you could try giving them something to carry to avoid them touching others or walls/objects/furniture. If the object is related to where the child is going (e.g. a ball when going to break time), this will also act as a visual cue and keep the child on task. A weighted/heavy object such as book or specially designed weighted toys (www.ldalearning.com) may also be beneficial as they provide additional body awareness, which is generally calming.

Sensitivity to textures

- **Grade the activity.** If a child has a sensitivity to handling particular textures, you may need to grade the activity as follows:
  - give the child a choice between two activities – the more control they have over the experience the more relaxed they will be and less likely to find it uncomfortable;
  - let them observe at first and gradually come closer to the activity area;
  - always allow the child to be in control – never push their hand into a texture or touch them with it without asking them.
  - Suggest they use just one finger to touch at first, then two fingers and gradually increase the surface area of the hand/skin that is in contact with the texture.
  - Allow them to only do one part of the activity. For example, with a sticking activity they may be able to stick the piece on if someone else applies the glue.
- **Providing utensils where appropriate.** If the child can't tolerate handling a particular material or texture, you might consider allowing them to use pincers or pegs or wear gloves to pick it up.
- **Wiping face.** The lips and face are especially sensitive.
  - Encourage the child to do as much as possible for themselves as they will be less sensitive to their own touch.
  - Ask the child to use firm, dabbing strokes to clean the face with a dry napkin.
  - If the face is not sufficiently clean, water or a wet wipe is required. Have a dry towel to hand to allow the child to dry their face afterwards.
- **Adapted uniform.** If the child finds their uniform hard to tolerate, discuss with the headteacher and parents about adapting it. It may be possible for the child to wear the PE uniform to school (especially on PE days to minimise stress caused by having to change) or they may be allowed to not wear part of the uniform, such as the tie or jumper, at the start of the year and gradually introduce it as their tolerance increases.

Aspect 3: Tactile (touch)

Aspect 3: Tactile (touch)

Letter	Touch from other people	Touching/handling objects or people	Sensitivity to textures
E	Comfortably stands at the back or front of a line with other children	With support, touches objects only when appropriate when sitting at a table	With prompting, wipes face clean after eating
E	With support, tolerates minimal accidental touch within the classroom (e.g. being bumped into)	With prompting, touches objects only when appropriate when sitting at a table	With support, calms down after a minor injury (e.g. a bump or scrape) within 5 minutes
F	Tolerates occasional unexpected touch from others (e.g. a peer tapping them to get their attention)	Touches objects only when appropriate when sitting at a table	Tolerates cleaning hands and face when necessary
F	Comfortably stands anywhere in a line and moves into the classroom	With prompting, uses touch appropriately with others	With support, calms down after a minor injury (e.g. a bump or scrape) within 1-2 minutes
G	Tolerates unexpected touch from others when moving in the classroom	With prompting, uses touch appropriately	Notices and cleans own face and hands after eating
G	Tolerates unexpected touch from others when moving in a busy environment (e.g. a corridor)	Uses touch appropriately (e.g. to get someone's attention)	Shows appropriate response to pain

Suggested activities or strategies

Touch from other people

- **Human Pretzel.** Deep pressure to the skin has a calming effect on the tactile system.
  - The child sits on a chair with feet flat on the floor.
  - Ask them to cross one leg over the other and then wrap the foot of the top leg behind the ankle, so the legs look twisted together like a pretzel.
  - Do the same with the arms – ask the child to cross one over the other and wrap the hands around the shoulders to give themselves a hug.
  - Ask the child to squeeze themselves tightly.
  - Swap the cross of the arms and legs and repeat.
- **Hand cushion.** Ask the child to put their hands under their legs to apply deep pressure to the hands for 10 seconds; this may decrease sensitivity to touch.

Touching/handling objects or people

- **Social Stories™.** If the child has difficulty knowing when it is appropriate to touch others, use social stories to explain this and reinforce with praise when the child gets it right.
- **Quiet hands.** Use a phrase (e.g. '*Quiet hands*' or '*Hands down*') to prompt the child to stop touching another child if it's not appropriate.
- **Visual cue.**
  - During a PE activity, ask each child to stand inside a hoop. Demonstrate how they can't reach each other without stepping out of their hoop.
  - Explain that we have to pretend that we have a hoop around us in the class too, so we must all keep our hands within our own circle.
  - In class, prompt children by saying '*Hands in your own circle*'/'*hoola hoop Jane*'.
- **Positioning.** You may need to leave a bigger distance between the child and another child to discourage them from touching the other child.

- **Arm's length.** Teach the child to leave a bigger distance between themselves and the child in front, for example, by giving a spacing cue such as '*arm's length*' when standing in line.
- **Fidgets.** Allowing a child to hold an item that meets their sensory needs can help them to pay attention by providing calming tactile input. It also might stop the child fidgeting with other items on the table or their neighbour's table, which might be more of a distraction. Specially designed fidget toys (www.ldalearning.com) can be used, or a piece of Blu Tack®, a stress ball or sticking a textured strip on the desk (like the soft side of Velcro®) can be used.

Sensitivity to textures

- **Graded play activities** to encourage tactile processing. You can encourage the child to explore different textures using the following activity.
  - Fill containers with different dry substances (e.g. sand, rice or uncooked pasta).
  - Place a number of small items in the container (such as Lego™ pieces) and the child has to find them with their eyes closed.
  - Allow them to use pincers at first, then progress to using hands.
  - Reverse roles and ask them to hide the objects for you to find. For more touch games see Sensory Shuffle at www.ldalearning.com.

Aspect 3: Tactile (touch)

Aspect 4: Vestibular (movement and balance)

Letter	Seeking movement	Tolerance of movement	Posture	Balance
A	Following a movement break, stands to complete a 3–5 minute activity at a table	Tolerates a busy environment with other people moving when they are still	Sits upright with support from walls/a chair back for 3–5 minutes	With support, balances when seated cross-legged on the floor for 3–5 minutes
A	Following a movement break, sits still at a table for 5 minutes in order to complete an activity	With support, walks slowly in a calm environment	With support from a wall or person, adopts an upright posture whilst standing for 1–2 minutes	With support, balances when seated and reaching for something arm's distance away
B	Following a movement break, stands for 10 minutes to complete an activity at a table	Tolerates a busy environment with other people moving quickly when they are walking slowly	With support and prompting, corrects posture momentarily	Balances when seated on the floor cross-legged
B	Following a movement break, sits still at a table for 10 minutes in order to complete an activity	Moves independently when walking slowly in all environments	With support and prompting, adopts an upright posture when seated for 5 minutes	Balances when seated and reaching for something arm's distance away
C	Following a movement break, stands to complete an activity at a table for up to 15 minutes	With support, moves quickly (e.g. jogging, running)	With support and prompting, maintains an upright posture when seated for 10 minutes	With support, balances on a chair when seated and looking forward
C	With support, remains seated for a short activity (5 minutes) without additional movement breaks	With support, moves slowly in one direction (e.g. up and down)	With prompting, maintains an upright posture in a chair during an activity	Maintains balance on a chair when seated still and looking forward
D	With support, remains seated for a short activity (10 minutes) without additional movement breaks	Moves slowly in one direction (e.g. up and down)	With prompting, adopts an upright posture whilst seated for 10 minutes during an activity	With support, maintains balance on a chair when bending forward or turning head or reaching for something
D	With support, plays appropriately in the playground	Moves quickly in one direction (e.g. jumping)	With prompting, adopts an upright posture whilst standing for 10 minutes during an activity	Maintains balance on a chair when bending forwards, turning head and/or reaching for something

Suggested activities or strategies*

Seeking movement

- **Movement breaks.** If a child is having difficulty remaining seated, try to incorporate movement into the activities they are doing. This could be through jobs in the classroom (e.g. handing out pencils), jobs outside of the classroom (e.g. taking messages), or scheduled movement breaks.
- **Let's go swimming** (Drew & Atter, 2009). The children sit well back in their chairs and pretend to go swimming. Ask them to move their arms and legs like the different swimming strokes: doggy paddle, breast stroke, back stroke, front crawl and butterfly.
- **Chair stretch.** Sometimes a simple chair stretch provides enough movement to help the child re-engage with the activity.
  - Ask the child to sit up in their chair with their feet flat on the ground.
  - Ask them to raise their arms above their head and reach for the ceiling.
  - Say '*Stretch as far as you can go*', then point their toes away from their body and stretch.
  - With the child's feet back on the floor, lean all the way down to touch their toes and drop their head down to look at the floor.
  - As they breathe in, sit up again and stretch their arms above your head and look all the way up at the ceiling.
  - Let go and come back to facing forward.

Tolerance of movement

Some children can be overly sensitive to movement and fear unstable surfaces for walking on (e.g. grass or sand), or avoid moving play equipment (e.g swings or slides). In more severe cases a child may even find looking at others moving difficult to tolerate. To build up a child's tolerance for movement, try practising at a quiet time. This way they won't fear being laughed at by peers or being accidently pushed or moved.

- **Melt.** Ask the children to stand up away from their chairs and pretend they are ice pops melting in the sun. Starting from the head, ask them to bend forward really slowly.
  - First tuck the chin into the chest then gradually bend from the waist until the hands are touching the toes and hanging loosely. Slowly uncurl.

Posture

- **Physical activity.** Activities that stimulate the vestibular system (i.e. involve movement) and strengthen the core muscles (muscles around the tummy and sides) will improve posture. Programmes such as the Smart Moves (www.smartcc.co.uk/smart-smartmoves.html) provide activities suitable for use in school.
- **Fragile egg.** (Henry D, 2005). Start in a sitting position on a mat. Ask them to curl up like a ball with their arms around their knees and chin tucked in to chest. Ask them to rock backwards and forwards without 'cracking the egg', i.e. extending the arms and legs.
- **Chair crunches.** Strengthening the core (tummy) muscles will help improve posture. Start with the children sitting well back in their chairs away from the table.
  - Ask them to lift their right leg off the floor.
  - Ask them to touch their left elbow to their right knee.
  - Change sides (right elbow to left knee).
  - Increase the number of chair crunches.

Balance

- **Compass.** Begin cross-legged on a mat. Ask the child to stretch their arms above their head and sit up as tall as possible. Ask them to lean as far forward as they can without tipping over (North), backwards (South), to the right (East) and to the left (West). Repeat faster using the rhyme '*North, South, East, West, I'm the kid that does my best*'.
- **Balance and aim.** Ask the child to sit on an inflated cushion or on a gym ball with their feet flat on the ground. Place beanbags on the floor around the child, and ask them to bend down and pick them up one at a time and shoot them into a target in front of them, such as a bucket or a hoop.

Aspect 4: Vestibular (movement and balance)

*For more movement and balance activities see 'Sensory games and activities' on pages 25–27.

Aspect 4: Vestibular (movement and balance)

Letter	Seeking movement	Tolerance of movement	Posture	Balance
E	With prompting, remains seated for long enough to complete a task	With support, moves quickly in all directions (e.g. running)	With prompting, maintains an upright posture for up to 15 minutes during an activity	With support, balances when standing
E	Plays on playground appropriately (e.g. does not seek out excessive movement)	Tolerates movement on fast-moving equipment in all directions (e.g. swings, slides)	With support and prompting, momentarily adopts an upright posture in standing	Balances when moving around the class for normal activities
F	Remains seated for long enough to complete a task	Moves quickly in all directions (e.g. running, jumping)	With prompting, maintains an upright posture when standing for up to 20 minutes during an activity	Balances when walking around the school avoiding obstacles
F	Moves in classroom appropriately (e.g. does not seek out excessive movement)	Moves quickly in all directions whilst others are moving slowly around them	Maintains an upright posture when standing for up to 10 minutes during an activity	Balances when moving quickly in one direction (e.g. running on the playground or during PE)
G	Remains seated for all classroom activities between normal school breaks	Moves quickly in all directions whilst others are also moving quickly around them	Maintains an upright posture when standing for approx. 20 minutes during an activity	Balances when moving quickly and changing direction

© Inés Lawlor 2017   *Target Ladders: Sensory Processing*   LDA   Permission to photocopy

Suggested activities or strategies*

Seeking movement

- **Work stations.** Think about ways that the children can move within the lesson. This could be by creating different work stations that they rotate through in small groups. Allow the children to choose which position they prefer to be in for some activities (e.g. sitting or lying on a chair or mat, or standing).
- **Spelling.** When teaching spelling of a new word, each child is given one letter of the alphabet. Call out the word, and the children have to spell it by the children with the correct letters standing up in the correct order and calling out their letter.
- **Seating.** Ensure the child's feet can reach the floor as all children will swing and slide on their seats if they can't touch the ground for stability. If not, use books or a wooden block under their feet. The occupational therapist working with the child might also recommend specialised seating such as a Movin' Sit cushion (www.ldalearning.com) or a ball seat (www.amazon.co.uk) if appropriate.

Tolerance of movement

- **Movement games.** If the child is engaged in a game and having fun, they are more likely to challenge themselves physically. You may consider using PE or playground time to build up the child's tolerance for movement through play. Resources such as Sensory Shuffle (www.ldalearning.com) provide useful ideas. Traditional games such as tag, grandmother's footsteps, What's the time Mr Wolf?, leapfrog, and Duck, Duck, Goose, all encourage movement. You can grade any movement game as follows:
  ○ allow the child to watch first;
  ○ start with only two players;
  ○ have 'safe' spots – (e.g. have cushions/mats on the ground that the child walks between but is 'safe' on);
  ○ walk instead of run;
  ○ increase the time playing gradually.
- **Mexican wave.** Start a Mexican wave around the class, where each child stands up one at a time in turns.
- **Lily pads.** Using two hoops per child the children have to travel from one end of the hall to the other, only stepping in the hoops.
- **Hoop relay.** Ask the child to stand in one hoop with another hoop in front of them. Ask them to bend down and lift the hoop over their head then step into the second hoop. They then place the first hoop in front of them and so on. This game could be played as a relay/race.

Posture

- **Prompting.** Sometimes a verbal prompt can remind a child to sit up straight if they are not aware that they are slumped. Show the child the difference between 'happy back' (upright) and 'sad back' (slumped), and prompt them at the start of an activity by saying *'happy backs'*. However, the child will find this increasingly tiring over time if they do not get an opportunity to move.
- **Beanbag balance.** The children sit upright in their seats. Give each child a beanbag. Ask them to sit upright and balance the beanbag on their head. See how long they can keep it on their heads without it slipping. Try different parts of the body (e.g. each foot lifted off the floor, their outstretched arm, on their back in an all fours position, etc.).
- **Cheerleader.** The children are given a word and have to spell it by making the shape with their bodies. The teacher says, for example, *'Give me a C, Give me an A, Give me a T. What does it spell?'* After each letter, the teacher calls the children to try and form that shape with their bodies, either sitting or standing.

Balance

- **Practise during PE.** Again, activities to develop balance are usually more suitable for PE or the playground as they involve movement. The child may need to lean on your shoulder in order to feel confident to attempt an activity. Whilst it is accepted that the long-term goal is independence in physical skills, if the child is at risk of falling, offering some physical assistance will help to keep them engaged in the activity and more motivated to improve.

Aspect 4: Vestibular (movement and balance)

*For more movement and balance activities see 'Sensory games and activities' on pages 25–27.

© Inés Lawlor 2017   *Target Ladders: Sensory Processing*   LDA   Permission to photocopy

Aspect 5: Proprioception (body awareness)

Letter	Co-ordinating movement	Personal space	Grading of force
A	With support, copies/mirrors simple movements in PE	With support, maintains appropriate personal space when sitting at a table	With support, grades the amount of force needed for picking up objects
A	With physical assistance, follows instructions to complete simple motor tasks (e.g. standing on one leg)	With prompting, maintains appropriate personal space when sitting at a table	With support, grips pencil with appropriate pressure
B	Copies/mirrors simple actions	With support, maintains appropriate personal space when standing in line	With prompting, grades the amount of force needed for picking up objects
B	With verbal cues, completes structured motor tasks (e.g. hopping)	With prompting, maintains appropriate personal space when standing in line	With prompting, grips pencil with appropriate pressure
C	With support, moves their body to complete structured two-part movements (e.g. hopscotch)	Maintains personal space when sitting at a table	Grades the amount of force needed for picking up an object
C	With support, moves around school without seeking out additional body awareness activities (e.g. bumping/crashing/leaning/stomping)	Maintains personal space when standing in line	With support, grades the pressure on the page needed when writing their name

© Inés Lawlor 2017 *Target Ladders: Sensory Processing* LDA Permission to photocopy

Suggested activities or strategies

Co-ordinating movement*

- If the child has difficulty in co-ordinating their body due to poor body awareness, it can lead to them feeling embarrassed and having low self-esteem. They may then withdraw from physical activity which leads to further delay in motor skills and other complications such as obesity. It is important that this is avoided where possible. Try motivating the child to keep trying through rewards such as stickers. Grade the activities where possible to make sure the child achieves.
- **Simon Says.** Show the child the movement at first, then build up to increase the difficulty by asking the child to do two-part movements or touch a different part of the body with each hand.
- **Mirror mirror.** Stand facing the child and ask them to pretend to be your mirror. Move slowly and ask them to copy your movements (e.g. arms above your head, arms to the side). Make it more difficult by asking them to repeat the movement with their eyes closed.

Personal space

- **Resistance.** Any activity where the child is actively using their muscles against resistance will improve body awareness. For example, carrying heavy books or putting the chairs up on the table provide proprioception. Activities to improve body awareness should be built into the routine if the child seems to be constantly seeking body awareness through stretching or bumping/crashing type activities. Carrying heavy things, chair stretches or push-ups are examples (already discussed). Try to incorporate opportunities to stretch and move between every activity (around every 20 minutes), then you can decrease as appropriate. If the child especially seems to seek out proprioception when moving (e.g. tapping the wall, stamping feet) try giving them something heavy to carry on the way (e.g. books or their school bag). Note that the weight should be no more than 10–15 per cent of the child's body weight to avoid injury (O'Connor, 2012). The child's occupational therapist may also recommend specialist weighted items, such as a weighted vest, lap pad or weighted blanket to use at intervals throughout the day (www.ldalearning.com).
- **Seating posture.** Again, check the child is well supported in the seat as this will provide them with more body awareness through being in contact with the seat, floor, backrest and armrests. If more supportive school chairs are available (e.g. with armrests), use these where possible. If not, consult the child's occupational therapists about recommending specialised seating.
- **Praise.** Prompt the child and praise them when they get it right (e.g. *'Well done for staying on your side of the table.'*).
- **Visual cues.** If needed, use visual cues to mark the area where the child should remain (e.g. taping a line down the table in coloured tape or giving the children a coloured circle/cushion to sit on during carpet time). Ideally, do the same for the whole class, so as not to single out the child with sensory issues. It will help others too.

Grading of force**

Children with SPD often find it difficult to judge the correct amount of force or pressure to use when handling objects. They often apply too much or too little pressure on the page when writing, for example, causing pain or discomfort in the hands.

The following activities can be used to build proprioception in the hands:

- **Twinkle twinkle little star.** Ask the child to make a fist then open the fingers out quickly. Repeat ten times.
- **Air piano.** Ask the child to pretend to play the piano, tapping each finger and thumb once then twice then three times starting with the thumb. Repeat, starting with the little finger.
- **Finger wrestle.** Ask the child to link their two index fingers together and gently pull each finger away from the other to separate them. Repeat with each pair of fingers.

*For more co-ordinating movement activities see 'Sensory games and activities' on page 26.
**For more grading of force activities see 'Sensory games and activities' on page 27.

© Inés Lawlor 2017   *Target Ladders: Sensory Processing*   LDA   Permission to photocopy

Aspect 5: Proprioception (body awareness)

Letter	Co-ordinating movement	Personal space	Grading of force
D	With support, stands in line without seeking out additional body awareness activities (e.g. bumping/crashing/leaning on objects or people)	With support, maintains appropriate personal space during parallel play	With support, grades the amount of force needed for physical play (e.g. when playing tag)
D	With support, attends to classroom activities without seeking out additional body awareness activities (e.g. bumping/crashing/leaning on objects or people)	With prompting, maintains appropriate personal space during parallel play	With prompting, uses appropriate pressure on the page when writing their name
E	With support, positions themselves and moves body when performing structured motor tasks during PE	With prompting, maintains appropriate personal space when sharing a toy with one other child	With prompting, grades the amount of force needed for physical play with others (e.g. when playing tag)
E	Positions themselves and moves body when performing structured motor tasks (e.g. forward rolls, hopscotch, PE activities)	With support, maintains appropriate personal space during a stationary group activity (e.g. story time)	Uses appropriate pressure on the page when writing their name
F	Moves around school without seeking out additional body awareness activities (e.g. bumping/crashing/leaning/stomping)	Maintains appropriate personal space during parallel play	Grades the amount of force needed for physical play with others (e.g. when playing tag)
F	Stands in line without seeking out additional body awareness activities (e.g. bumping/crashing/leaning on objects or people)	With prompting, maintains appropriate personal space during a group activity	Uses appropriate pressure on the page when writing a paragraph of writing
G	Positions themselves and moves body when playing movement games on the playground (e.g. running, hopping)	With support, maintains appropriate personal space during group games at break time	Grades the amount of force needed for all activities
G	Co-ordinates body with smooth movements whilst following rules as part of team ball games (e.g. football)	With prompting, maintains appropriate personal space during group games at break time	Consistently uses appropriate pressure on the page when performing a writing task
G	Attends to classroom activities without seeking out additional body awareness activities (e.g. bumping/crashing/leaning on objects or people)	Maintains appropriate personal space during all types of play	Grips pencil/pen with appropriate pressure

Suggested activities or strategies

Co-ordinating movement*

- **PE activities** that involve stretching, climbing, pushing or pulling will assist in developing body awareness through providing feedback through the muscles and joints.
- **Isometrics (sitting)**
  - Ask the child to put their hands together in a prayer position and push as hard as they can for a count of three. Release, shake out the hands and repeat three times.
  - Next, clasp the fingers together and pretend they are stuck with glue and try to pull them apart. Release, shake out the hands and repeat three times.
  - Place one foot on top of the other – press the top foot down and push up with the foot underneath. Hold for three then shake out the feet and swap the feet over, so the one that was on top is now on the bottom.
- **Wall push-ups.** Other common activities to use in the classroom are wall push-ups (child pushes against the wall) or chair push-ups (Henry D, 2000).
  - The child sits with their feet flat on the ground.
  - They hold on to the edge of their seat and lift their bottom off the seat and hold for a count of three, before repeating three times.

Personal space

It is common for children with poor body awareness to lack personal space and get closer to others than is socially appropriate. As they struggle to have a good sense of where their own body is, it can be difficult to know when they are too close to someone else.

- **Social Stories™.** Use social stories (www.carolgraysocialstories.com). If a child is having an issue with personal space in a particular context, try creating a social story for that context (e.g. standing in line, or talking to someone).
- **Visual cues.** It might be helpful to use a distance that the child can measure easily, such as 'arm's length'. You can teach the children about standing an arm's length from each other when lining up and then prompt them when needed if anyone is standing too close to someone else.
- **Over the head.** Body awareness can also be taught with a simple games such as 'over the head'.
  - Stand children in a line.
  - Give the first child a balloon and ask them to hand to the next child by putting it over their heads, using both hands.
  - Ask the next child where they will have to stand to receive the balloon without reaching forwards or bending backwards to avoid being hit. Challenge the rest of the class to stand where they think they will need to stand in order to receive the balloon.
  - Confirm that this is an appropriate spacing for lining up.

Grading of force**

- Theraputty (www.ldalearning.com) or playdough can be used to provide resistance to the muscles of the hands to improve strength and proprioception. The following activities are recommended:

Whole-hand squeeze
  - Use a tennis ball-size piece of putty, asking the child to place it in the palm of their hand and squeeze the putty with all four fingers and thumb. Repeat three times and with the other hand.

Thumb and index finger pinch
  - Break off a table tennis ball-size piece of putty and roll it into a 'snake' by using both hands together on the table.
  - Use the thumb and index finger of each hand to pinch along the length of the theraputty snake. Then, use the thumb and index finger to break off small pieces (pea size) and roll them between the thumb and index finger to make small spheres.

In-hand manipulation
  - See how quickly the child can pick all the pieces up with one hand with their thumb and index finger whilst holding the ones they've already picked up.

*For more co-ordinating movement activities see 'Sensory games and activities' on page 26.
**For more grading of force activities see 'Sensory games and activities' on page 27.

Aspect 6: Gustatory and olfactory (taste and smell)

Letter	Tolerating smell	Seeking sensation	Varying diet
A	With support/accommodation, tolerates day-to-day smells in the classroom	With support and using a suitable chewable toy, attends to class activities with constant use of item in the mouth	With support, eats the same lunch every day in a quiet space away from other children
A	Tolerates day-to-day smells in classroom	With prompting and using a suitable chewable toy, attends to class activities with constant use of item in the mouth	With support, will taste one new food once a week in a quiet space away from other children
A	With support/accommodation, tolerates strong smells around the school	With support and using a suitable chewable toy, attends to class activities with frequent use of item in the mouth	With encouragement, eats the same lunch every day in a quiet space away from other children
A	With support/accommodation, tolerates smells in a quiet space with others eating lunch	With prompting and using a suitable chewable toy, attends to class activities with frequent use of item in the mouth	With support, will try one new food each day in a quiet space away from other children
B	Tolerates strong smells in classroom (e.g. glue)	Uses a suitable chewable toy at regular intervals to maintain attention	With support, eats the same lunch every day in a quiet space with up to three other children
B	Tolerates strong smells in a quiet space with others eating lunch	By chewing on gum or a chewy snack at intervals, attends to lessons	With support, will try new food in their lunch box when sitting with a small group of children
C	With prior preparation, tolerates food smells in the canteen/dining hall for a short time (e.g. 5–10 minutes)	With prompting, attends to class activities without putting non-food objects in their mouth	Eats lunch every day in a quiet space with a small group of up to three other children
C	Tolerates food smells in the canteen/dining hall for a short time (e.g. 5–10 minutes)	With support, takes regular drinks from a water bottle to maintain attention	With support, sits in the canteen with other children having lunch
C	Tolerates strong food smells in the canteen/dining hall for the duration of lunchtime	By taking regular drinks from a water bottle, maintains attention	With support, eats own lunch in the canteen at the same time as other children
C	Tolerates strong smells (e.g. toilets) around school	Attends to class activities without putting non-food objects in their mouth, including a water bottle (unless they are thirsty)	Eats their own lunch in the canteen at the same time as other children

Suggested activities or strategies

Tolerating smell

- **Prepare the child.** If there is a particular smell the child dislikes (e.g. fish) and it is always served on a certain day, then prepare the child in advance (e.g. by using a visual timetable).
- **Graded exposure.** Gradually increase the child's exposure to the environment/product that they do not like the smell of. If they have a strong dislike of a particular smell, their reaction may be so strong it might cause them to gag, so it will be impossible for them to eat their own lunch in this environment. Start by allowing the child to eat their lunch in another room and gradually increase the length of time they spend in the dining hall after having eaten their own lunch. If possible, gradually introduce them to eating in the dining hall.
- **Use Social Stories™.** Teach the child how to respond appropriately if they find a smell offensive, using social stories or role-play. The child may genuinely feel sick at a particular smell, but it might cause offence if it is another child's lunch! Suggest moving away or saying '*I don't really like …*' rather than '*That's disgusting*', which could be upsetting for another child.

Seeking sensation

Chewing or sucking can help a child pay attention, and it can also be calming if a child is too alert. Adults often chew their pen top when concentrating or bite their nails when nervous, while a child might chew school equipment or their school uniform.

- **Replace it with something they *can* chew.** If the child needs to chew something when concentrating, try replacing the items you don't want them to chew with something they are allowed to chew. There are products designed for chewing (e.g. chewellry/chewy tubes – www.ldalearning.com) which the parents or school might consider purchasing. The child's occupational therapist or speech and language therapist can help you choose a suitable one if needed. If the child tends to chew the pencil top, purchase a chew top for the pencil; if they tend to chew their cuffs, a chew bracelet might be more suitable.
- If appropriate, consider allowing the child to chew **chewing gum** when concentrating on work. If this is not suitable at school, the parents might consider it during homework.
- **Water/sports bottle on desk.** Sucking is also generally calming. Allowing the child to keep a sports bottle on the table filled with water can provide this sensory input in a socially appropriate way. Very cold drinks are usually alerting; taking regular sips of cold water might help the child maintain attention to the task.
- **Prompting.** Regular prompting and praise for when the child uses the suitable chew item rather than the unsuitable item can help reinforce the behaviour and form new habits.
- Activities that involve **blowing or sucking** are usually calming to the sensory system. An example is 'table air football'.
  - Use a small piece of cotton wool or a small piece of paper rolled into a ball.
  - Sit across the table from the child.
  - Use straws to blow the cotton wool ball from one end of the table to the other and score a goal.

Varying diet

- **Visual timetables.** Place a preferred food or activity on the visual timetable after the child takes a taste of a new food. Say '*First this*' (new food) *and then…*'
- **Grade exposure to new foods**.
  - Allow the child to touch and smell the food only.
  - Allow the child to lick the food only.
  - Allow the child to take a tiny bite and spit it out if necessary.
  - Allow the child to eat only a tiny piece (i.e. a $\frac{1}{2}$ cm cube) of the food to get the reward.
  - Allow the child to choose between two new foods to taste.
  - Reward and praise all achievements.

Aspect 7: Interoception (internal body functions and emotions)

Letter	Emotional regulation	Hunger/thirst	Elimination
A	With support and a quiet environment, calms down within 30 minutes after becoming upset	With support, will eat and drink at regular intervals	Requires assistance to know when he/she has had an accident
A	With support and a quiet environment, calms down within 15 minutes after becoming upset	When prompted, eats and drinks at regular intervals	Knows when he/she has had an accident and requests assistance
A	Following an incident of being upset, discusses what happened (may get upset during recall)	Confirms if thirsty when asked	Goes to the toilet as part of a schedule every hour/$1\frac{1}{2}$ hours
A	With support, uses appropriate strategies to calm down when upset	Confirms if hungry when asked	With support (e.g. visual support), makes it to the toilet on time
B	With prompting, identifies when becoming upset	Identifies when thirsty and tells a teacher	With frequent prompting, goes to the toilet on time
B	Following an incident of being upset, discusses what happened without becoming upset again	Identifies when hungry and tells a teacher	With prompting at break times, goes to the toilet on time
C	If upset, with support and prompting, confirms what they are upset about in words	Identifies if hungry or thirsty and, with support, waits 10–15 minutes to eat or drink	Identifies the need to go to the toilet and makes it in time if allowed to go immediately
C	If upset, explains in words what they are upset about	Identifies if hungry or thirsty and waits 10–15 minutes to eat or drink	With support, waits up to 5 minutes to go to the toilet
D	When upset or hurt, calms down within a reasonable amount of time with minimal support	With support, waits until break time to eat or drink	With support, waits until a convenient moment (up to 15 minutes) to go to the toilet
D	Identifies when becoming upset and seeks support	Identifies when hungry or thirsty and waits until break time to eat or drink	Identifies the need to go to the toilet and waits until a convenient moment/break time to go

Suggested activities or strategies

Emotional regulation

As discussed earlier, children with SPD can be more prone to emotional outbursts or meltdowns due to sensory clashes with the environment they are in. Using the sensory strategies discussed already should help to avoid this. At times, the child is not aware that they are becoming upset until they are at the point of a meltdown. If this happens, use the strategies outlined earlier in this book to calm the child as quickly as possible.

- **Teach strategies at a time when calm**. When the child is calm, teach strategies to calm down if they become upset. Teaching breathing techniques, going to a quiet space and sensory strategies such as wall push-ups would be helpful (see the chapter on creating a sensory-friendly classroom on pages 24–34).
- **Give the child a system** to indicate when they are feeling upset. During a meltdown, it can be difficult for the child to ask for what they want or explain what is happening to them. Consider giving the child a picture card saying '*I need help*' or '*I need a break*'. By encouraging the child to use the card rather than other inappropriate methods, such as screaming, crying, hitting, etc., they can gradually learn to use the card before becoming upset. Traffic light signals (www.ldalearning.com) can also be used to help the child communicate that the environment is becoming too stressful. If the child does not understand at first how to use the cards, you can prompt them when you notice that they are first becoming upset. Hand the child the card as you say the words on the card (e.g. '*Do you need some help?*'). Praise and reward the child for using the strategies.

Hunger/thirst

A child with SPD may not perceive they are hungry or thirsty. Combined with food sensitivity, they may actually eat and drink very little. Understandably, this can make it very difficult for the child to attend to class work if they are hungry or thirsty.

- **Offer snacks or drinks**. If the child appears to be becoming upset or losing attention, offer a snack or drink of water if it has been a while since break time.
- **Modify the environment**. Make the environment as 'sensory friendly' as possible (see previous Target Ladders) to ensure the child eats and drinks at break times.

Elimination

Difficulties with toileting are common in children with sensory issues. Often, they do not register the need to go to the toilet until it is too late, or feel uncomfortable and become agitated or upset when they need the toilet. Discuss with the parents strategies that they are implementing at home, so they are consistent with strategies used in school too.

- **Read body language**. Sometimes the child's body language will reflect the need to go to the toilet even if they are not aware of it. Prompt the child '*Do you need to go to the toilet?*'.
- **Schedule**. If a child has frequent accidents, it may be useful to take them to the toilet at regular intervals (every $1\frac{1}{2}$–2 hours) or more frequently if needed. If they use the toilet and stay dry, reward and praise the child.
- **Language**. If a child is getting strong signals to use the toilet, they may find it difficult to communicate this to you. Giving them a set phrase '*Toilet break please*' or a 'toilet pass' card that they can bring up to you might help get them to the toilet on time.

Making changes brainstorming sheet

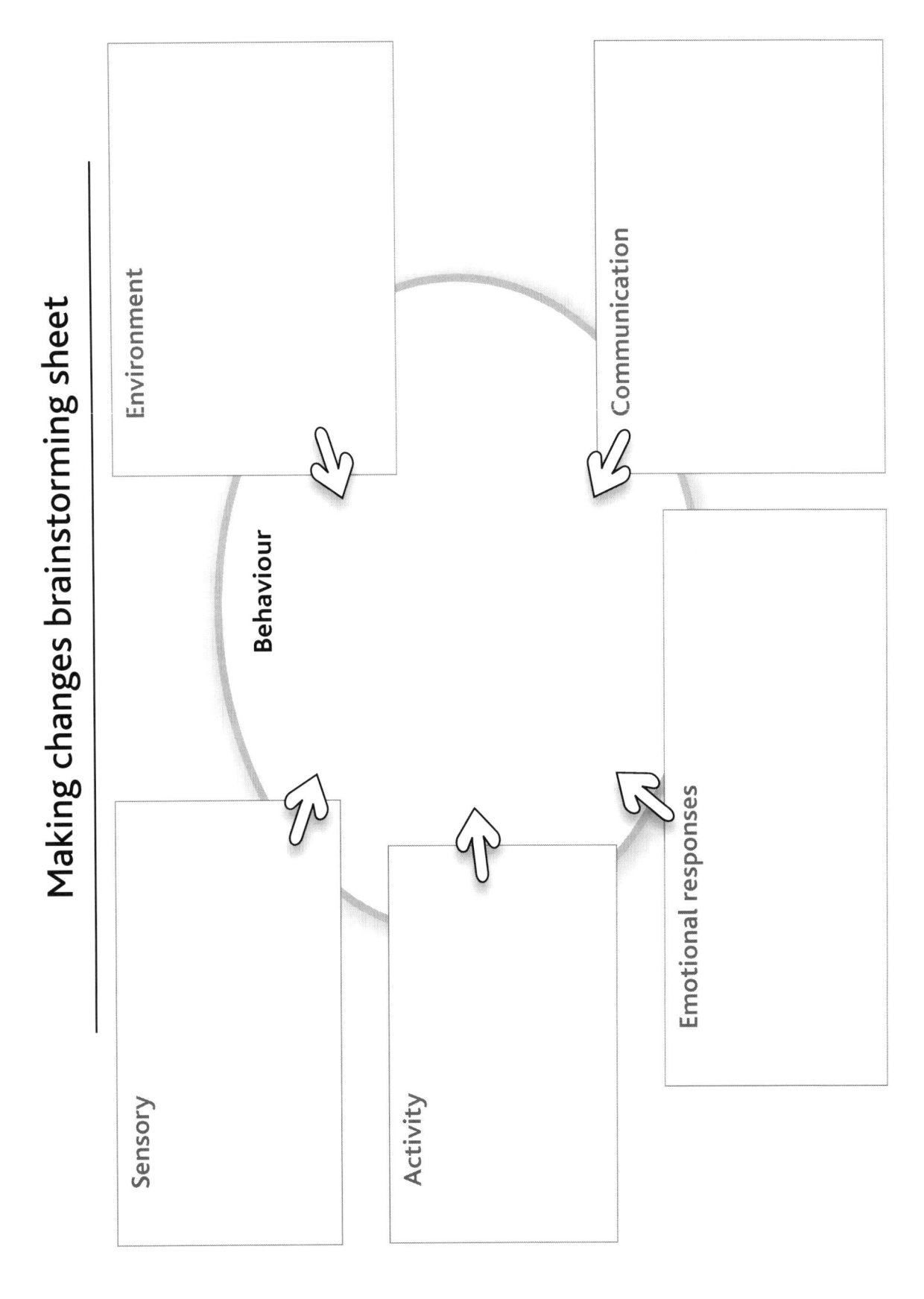

- Environment
- Communication
- Emotional responses
- Activity
- Sensory

Behaviour

© Inés Lawlor 2017   *Target Ladders: Sensory Processing*   LDA   Permission to photocopy

References

Addy L (2016). How to support pupils with sensory processing needs. Hyde. LDA.

American Psychiatric Association (2013). Diagnostic and statistical manual of mental disorders (DSM-5™). Arlington, Texas. American Psychiatric Publishing.

Ayres AJ (1972). Sensory integration and learning disorders. Los Angeles, California. Western Psychological Services.

Bundy A, Lane S & Murray E (2002). Sensory integration theory and practice. 2nd edn. Philadelphia, Pennsylvania. FA Davis Company.

Biel L & Peske N (2009). Raising a sensory smart child: the definitive handbook for helping your child with sensory processing issues. London. Penguin Books.

Children and Families Act 2014. London. HMSO.

Department for Education (2015). Special educational needs and disability code of practice: 0 to 25 years. London. HMSO.

Drew S & Atter L (2009). Fidget busters: brain breaks and energisers for the classroom. Hyde. LDA.

Dunn W (2015). Sensory profile 2™. www.pearsonclinical.co.uk

Gabriels R, Agnew J & Miller L (2008). 'Is there a relationship between restricted, repetitive, stereotyped behaviours and interests and abnormal sensory response in children with autism spectrum disorder?' In *Autism Spectrum Disorders 2* (4): 660-70.

Greene R (2014a). The explosive child: a new approach for understanding and parenting easily frustrated, chronically inflexible children. New York. Harper.

Greene R (2014b) Lost at school: why our kids with behavioral challenges are falling through the cracks and how we can help them. New York. Scribner.

Hanscom A (2016). Balanced and barefoot: how unrestricted outdoor play makes for strong, confident, and capable children. Oakland, California. New Harbinger Publications.

Henry D (2000). Tool chest for teachers, parents and students: a handbook to facilitate self-regulation. Santa Barbara, California. Henry Occupational Therapy Services, Inc.

Lane S (2002). Chapter 4: Sensory Modulation. In Bundy A, Lane S & Murray E (2002). Sensory integration theory and practice. 2nd edn. Philadelphia, Pennsylvania. FA Davis Company.

Landy J & Burridge K (1999). Ready-to-use fine motor skills and handwriting activities: teaching, remediation and assessment. New York. Centre for Applied Research in Education.

Lawlor I (2016). Max and me: a story about sensory processing. Dublin. www.mymodulator.com

Lyon S et al (2014). Speech, language and communication needs. Hyde. LDA.

Mahler K (2016). www.aapcpublishing.net/the-outlook/interoception-the-eighth-sensory-system.aspx

Miller L (2014). Sensational kids: hope and help for children with sensory processing disorder. New York. Penguin Random House.

Miller L, Nielsen D & Schoen S (2012). Attention deficit hyperactivity disorder and sensory modulation disorder: a comparison of behaviour and physiology. In *Research in Developmental Disabilities*, *33* (3): 804-18.

Myles et al (2000). Asperger syndrome and sensory issues: practical solutions for making sense of the world. Shawnee Mission, Kansas. Autism Asperger Publishing Company.

O'Connor C (2012). Success in school: how to help children pay attention and concentrate in the classroom and improve kids, focus on homework – a guide for parents and teachers. Co. Galway. Roundstone.

Parham LD et al (2007). Sensory processing measure manual. Los Angeles, California. Western Psychological Services.

Roley S, Blanche E & Schaaf R (2001). Understanding the nature of sensory integration with diverse populations. Philadelphia, Pennsylvania. Therapy Skills Builders®: A Harcourt Health Sciences Company.

Wilbarger P (1984). Planning an adequate 'sensory diet': application of sensory processing theory during the first year of life. In *Zero to Three, 5* (1), September: 7–12.

Williams M & Shellenberger S (1996). How does your engine run?: a leader's guide to the alert program for self-regulation. Albuquerque, New Mexico. Therapyworks, Inc.

Links to other *Target Ladders* titles

Target Ladders: Behavioural, Emotional and Social Difficulties
Rachel Foulger, Sue Smallwood and Marion Aust

Includes additional targets for:
- Controlling emotions;
- Taking responsibility;
- Social interactions with peers;
- Managing transitions.

Target Ladders: Autistic Spectrum
Louise Nelson

Includes additional targets for:
- Social interaction – friendships and relationships;
- Managing change;
- Personal organisation;
- Managing feelings;
- Non-verbal interaction.

Target Ladders: Visual Perception
Mark Hill

Includes additional targets for:
- Visual memory and skills;
- Visual sequential memory;
- Visual motor integration.

Target Ladders: Speech, Language and Communication Needs
Susan Lyon et al.

Includes additional targets for:
- Attention control;
- Comprehension;
- Expressive language;
- Social communication;
- Phonological awareness, auditory discrimination and speech.

Target Ladders: Working Memory and Auditory Processing
Kate Ruttle

Includes additional targets for:
- Auditory processing and exploring sound;
- Auditory processing for communication;
- Visual-spatial memory;
- Kinaesthetic memory;
- Memory, attention and organisation.

Other useful resources

Fidget Busters: Brain Breaks and Energisers for the Classroom
Sharon Drew and Liz Atter

How to Support Pupils with Sensory Processing Needs
Lois Addy

Sensory Shuffle
Inés Lawlor

For more resources suitable for children with sensory processing difficulties, visit www.ldalearning.com